099227

JM 2/10

Creative Encounters

ns in science, n and the arts

Edited by
Ralph Levinson
Helen Nicholson
Simon Parry

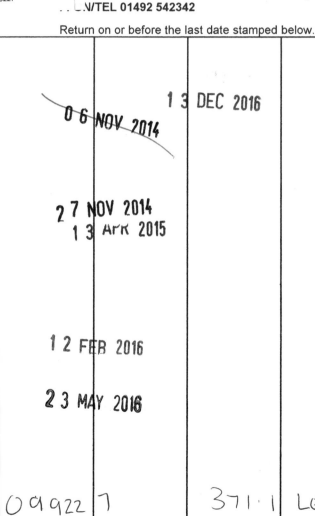

Creative Encounters
New conversations in science,
education and the arts

Editors:
Ralph Levinson
Helen Nicholson
Simon Parry

Consultant Editor: Ian Jones, Isinglass
Consultancy

Illustration: Edvard Scott

ISBN 978 1 84129 077 5

First published by the Wellcome Trust, 2008.

The Wellcome Trust is the largest charity in the UK.
It funds innovative biomedical research, in the UK
and internationally, spending over £600 million
each year to support the brightest scientists with
the best ideas. The Wellcome Trust supports
public debate about biomedical research and its
impact on health and wellbeing.

www.wellcome.ac.uk

Wellcome Trust
Gibbs Building
215 Euston Road
London NW1 2BE

The Wellcome Trust is a charity registered in England, no.
210183. Its sole trustee is The Wellcome Trust Limited, a
company registered in England, no. 2711000, whose registered
office is at 215 Euston Road, London NW1 2BE, UK.

Contents

Foreword

Clare Matterson

It is almost 50 years since CP Snow commented upon what he saw as the divide between two cultures: artistic and scientific. This book offers an opportunity to consider that divide afresh and it would be intriguing to know what Snow would make of the situation today.

The editors of this book offer an optimistic perspective on the interplay between different disciplines and the benefits that can accrue from successful creative encounters – many funded through the Pulse and other strands of the Wellcome Trust's Engaging Science grants programme. In doing so they identify several cultures and demonstrate that, while the degree of disciplinary fragmentation may be much greater than in 1959, the extent of overlap between them is notable. In some ways this is recognition of the increasing complexity of the scientific world and the difficulty of establishing a single view of scientific endeavour. Equally, it raises the status of dialogue and activity between scientists and non-scientists from the status of 'nice to have' to 'essential'.

This is not to say that you will find within this book any universal truths about the ways in which formal and less formal approaches to science education and improving scientific literacy can be generated: indeed the authors are refreshingly candid about the challenges inherent in such collaborations. Nevertheless – this book is positive about the interplay between disciplines and is supportive of creating and finding teaching and learning opportunities in a variety of settings within and outwith classrooms.

Snow might well be dismayed to find that there are more and more scientific and artistic disciplines. However, it does not follow that this increasing variety leads to fewer opportunities to find 'creative' approaches to scientific understanding and 'scientific' approaches to creativity. This book does much to exemplify these opportunities and to showcase the best endeavours of professionals seeking to enhance the engagement between science and society.

Clare Matterson is Director of Medicine, Society and History at the Wellcome Trust.

Creative encounters: an introduction

In his study of the science of acting, Joseph Roach observes that 17th-century actors believed that an actor's passions were contagious: they could literally transform the audience's beliefs and moral values. In 21st-century London, the theatre director Katie Mitchell continues to investigate scientific understanding of the emotions in the immediacy of the rehearsal room. Drawn to the idea that emotions incite physical changes in the body, she has applied the work of the neuroscientist Antonio Damasio to the rehearsal process, thereby redefining the practices of acting through the study of science. Instances of scientific research influencing the arts are evident throughout history, just as scientists have drawn on metaphors and symbolism from the arts to describe their practices and processes. Science and the arts have informed each other by unfixing certainties, and by disturbing and challenging established modes of thought. Scientific and artistic experiments share a lack of linearity and certainty, although this way of thinking has not always been recognised in forms of education that have favoured rather more measurable and predictable outcomes.

This book is motivated by an ambition to reflect on the ways in which young people might explore the creative opportunities presented by collaborations between scientists and artists. Through a series of well-defined funding schemes that aimed to forge links between the arts, biomedical science and its ethical implications, the Wellcome Trust has had the opportunity to support young people's creative and critical engagement with socio-scientific subject matter. Detailed evaluations of these projects have raised broader issues about the ways in which science is perceived and understood by young people, the role of creativity in education and the power of collaboration to generate an enthusiasm for learning. The authors gathered together in this book have been invited to reflect on pedagogic questions raised by interdisciplinary educational practices, and to raise questions about the ways in which creative educational practices contribute to encouraging young people to become informed citizens. This introductory chapter explicitly addresses the place of creativity in education, the ways in which dominant narratives of science have become embedded in educational discourse and the popular imagination, and the concept and practice of citizenship.

It is impossible to fully document the rich dialogues between artists, educationalists and scientists that occur in genuinely creative collaborations. Embracing the complexities that lie at the heart of these experiences invites us to struggle with inherited beliefs and prejudices about the social roles of the arts and sciences in education, and to be open to new conceptualisations of the relationship between forms of knowing that have sometimes been caricatured as distanced, categorised as different and characterised as inherently distinctive. In an attempt to make a provisional map of this rocky territory, we have chosen to group the essays in this volume around three conceptual themes: Wonder, Space and Narrative. Each of these themes illuminates educational questions about the dynamic relationship between science, citizenship and creativity. Each recognises that learning takes place when young people are invited to make connections between the social and personal, when they become both emotionally involved with their work and make informed judgements about the ethics and practices of science.

The first section explores the idea of wonder, in which authors have focused on the importance of beauty and the aesthetic to the processes of learning, how the possibilities of biotechnology have been explored by artists to release the moral imagination, how play and illusion help develop new relationships that enhance interpretations of our experience. Relationships and interconnections are treated in the theme of space in the second section. Throughout the world, physical spaces in schools are being transformed, maximising collegiality and promoting new metaphors and discourses of learning. Intermingling of professional spaces between scientists and artists presents new opportunities for understanding illness, and performance in a hospital rather than the dedicated dramatic space of a theatre creates new forms of social participation. In the third section, on narrative and storytelling, we see how marginalised people have disrupted conventional science and educational discourses and have been able to tell their own authentic accounts of science. But we are also reminded that stories can be told through a variety of art forms, including dance, and that the process of creating and linking narratives in different forms is complex but rewarding.

Taken as a whole, this is a book that is intended to stimulate discussion and debate, to celebrate the creativity of those working in education and to raise provocative questions about how creative encounters between the arts and sciences might challenge young people's perceptions and ideas.

Encountering citizenship and science

The types of collaboration and partnership discussed above might seem distant to science teachers dealing with the content necessary for students to pass examinations. Science at school is often perceived as based on laws and theories that appear to yield solid facts and, if there are stories to tell, these are often about the heroic individuals who revealed the laws. The laws of thermodynamics, the gas laws, Newton's laws of motion and natural selection stand as true, impressive bulwarks of the authority of scientific knowledge. From a student's – and indeed teacher's – point of view it can seem that these simply have to be learned, and that they are very distant from the humanistic concerns that are the very stuff of the arts. But developments in medicine and the biosciences, together with unprecedented access to information through the world wide web, have created new possibilities of partnership, participation and dialogue such that the paternalistic model of deference to scientific expertise is no longer tenable (Layton *et al.*, 1993; Nowotony *et al.*, 2005). For example, identification of genetic conditions at preconception, pre-natal and post-natal stages have given urgency to ideas of rights, autonomy, personal risk and decision-making. The rights and identities of disabled people, the concept of disability, are particularly bound up with these developments. Citizens are no longer set apart from the science but those who seek to ensure such changes can be put to the advantage of the public have become scientific citizens (Michael and Brown, 2005).

In the practices discussed in this book there is a constant and dynamic entwining of an idea of science with an idea of citizenship. The counterpart to the scientific citizen mentioned above is the scientist as citizen. In his 1995 Nobel Prize acceptance speech, the eminent physicist and citizen-scientist Professor Joseph Rotblat told a story:

> Two wise men were arguing about the ancient civilization in their respective countries. One said: "my country has a long history of technological development: we have carried out deep excavations and found a wire, which shows that already in the old days we had the telegraph." The other man retorted: "we too made excavations; we dug much deeper than you and found…nothing, which proves that already in those days we had wireless communication!" (Rotblat, 1995)

Rotblat's story is illuminating in a number of ways. Although he was using the tale to refute the idea that the existence of nuclear weapons has prevented a world war since 1945, it also invites examination of the link between the history of civilisation and the history of technological development. It raises questions about the nature and genesis of ideas and evidence. It also encourages us to think about the connections between national narratives and the narrative of scientific progress.

Joseph Rotblat's personal narrative is equally enlightening. He left Poland shortly before Hitler's invasion and subsequently worked on the Manhattan Project developing the A-bomb. He later became a highly respected researcher of the applications of nuclear physics to medicine. However, his Nobel Prize was for peace not for science. From when he left the Manhattan Project at the end of the War, he devoted himself to activism, leading campaigns against nuclear arms proliferation until his death in 2005 at the age of 96. He was a passionate believer in the potential of science to create new knowledge and benefit humanity. However, he also asserted the responsibilities of scientists to think about how their work would impact on society, reminding them that "the ivory tower was finally demolished by the Hiroshima bomb" (Rotblat, 1995). He felt that developments in science and technology had the potential to bring people together but also brought new risks, which, in turn, required new loyalties that crossed national boundaries and gave new responsibilities to scientists and citizens. He could not separate his personal narrative from his professional life, nor could he separate his ideas about science from his ideas about citizenship. He promoted an idea of global citizenship as an explicit and necessary response to his understanding of scientific progress.

The exact nature of public fears in the nuclear age may seem a bit outdated now. However the challenges faced by the next generation of citizen-scientists and scientific citizens will be arguably even greater. In 2007 the Nobel Peace Prize was won by the Intergovernmental Panel on Climate Change (IPCC) jointly with Al Gore. The IPCC has been the focus for collaboration among thousands of scientists from all over the world. It has been driven by a recognition that to understand the phenomenon of climate change, imagine its implications and find ways to address these, it will require an unprecedented level of cooperation across borders and between disciplines. It will also require new understanding between scientists, policy makers and citizens.

This represents a clear challenge to policy makers, scientists and the public as a whole that is passed on to educators thinking about the demands that are facing future citizens. Not only do they have to find ways of educating future citizens and scientists to meet such demands, but a certain creative effort also has to go into imagining what these challenges might be. How can we prepare young people to negotiate the relationship between science and citizenship in the 21st century when we struggle to understand its relationship in the 20th? As the futurologists of education are fond of pointing out, we are educating for a world where 50 per cent of the jobs today's primary school children will do have not been invented yet. However, these are the questions that creative science educators are dealing with on a daily basis and it is with these questions that the authors in this book are grappling with either explicitly or implicitly.

The territory is complex. Just as the relationship between science and society is shifting, so notions of citizenship in most parts of the world are contested. In much of the West, there are strong traditions, reaching back to the Enlightenment, of citizenship as a set of rights of the individual embodied in the institutions of the nation-state. This conception, in its British post-World War II context, was succinctly and influentially described by the sociologist T H Marshall (1950). He traced back civil, political and social rights to their origins in the struggles of the 18th, 19th and 20th centuries and related them to the structures and provisions of postwar European social democracies with their independent legal systems, universal suffrage and developing welfare states. Parallel to this liberal tradition of thought run other, often competing, traditions based on collective belonging. Within communitarian thinking, group rights may take precedence over the rights of individual group members. Tensions between these ways of thinking arise frequently where the liberal precepts of the state, for instance around equal rights for all citizens, run counter to group restrictions on certain behaviours. Whether this results in conflict between the state and minority ethnic groups or between the state and supranational religious identities, loyalties of the citizen can be divided. Science frequently throws up such dilemmas. Government might deem the right to reproduction to be a universal one, or universal enough to provide IVF treatment through the welfare state. However, some religious groups might forbid its uptake by members on doctrinal grounds.

In addition to its contested context, in the 50 years since Marshall's work, the picture he painted has been complicated in many ways, not just by the influence of other traditions of political thought, but also in terms of the everyday experience of the citizen. In addition to concerns around climate change there is the acceleration in the development of communications technologies. We can now travel more, further and faster, have access to huge amounts of information and live within an endless torrent of media. While technological progress and increasing globalisation have touched most people's lives, they do not seem to have eliminated inequalities. The potential for global travel may be there and mass migration is a huge factor in creating the dynamic nature of the world we live in, but freedom of movement is seriously unequal, restricted to many without the right citizenship status. Communications technologies are spreading rapidly but are not available to all and the ubiquitous media can be as homogenising and as dismissive of diversity as they can be educational and empowering. Our understanding of citizenship must cope with an ever-changing context in which new arenas for the possession of rights are proliferating. In Marshall's day, rights had a past and a present but now we think more and more about their future. We have to address serious issues about the rights of the unborn child and where they start. We also have to look further ahead when considering the rights of future generations in relation to the environment. This proliferation of rights draws ever more attention to the unevenness of their possession. If a citizen of Japan born in 2004 is entitled to expect to live to 82, why is a citizen of Swaziland born in the same year only entitled to expect to live to 37?[1] This changing context is often explained in terms of an experience of a world compressed in space and time (Harvey). Just as future citizens will have to think across spatial, national and disciplinary boundaries, they will also need to think back into the past and forward into the future with a degree of flexibility and creativity. In response to this changing social and political climate, many activists and theorists are looking to conceptualise citizenship less as a set of rights and institutions and more as a set of practices. Melissa Leach and Ian Scoones, writing from the interdisciplinary perspective of science and development studies, have formulated a useful conception of citizenship that seems to encapsulate this idea as "practised engagement through emergent social solidarities" (Leach, 2005, p. 31).

In these challenging times, there are some welcome initiatives, such as the Intergovernmental Panel on Climate Change, that enable scientific experts to engage with each across national boundaries and form new social solidarities. However, what fora for engagement with scientific ideas are available to citizens outside the scientific community? How can members of the public develop solidarities with scientific experts? How might educators prepare young people for a citizenship that does not just include the passive retention of rights and an ability to navigate the institutions of the nation-state, but also encompasses citizenship as practical engagement? This is particularly crucial in relation to science, where the implications are rarely confined within national borders and where the perception is often that state institutions struggle to keep up with the pace of progress. How might one 'practise the practice' of citizenship in a safe space but with a strong sense of a connection to real-world problems? This is clearly a challenge but one to which many of the practices dealt with in this book have risen.

The Pulse projects provided opportunities for practical encounters with scientific aspects of citizenship, through what the Pulse

evaluation describes as the creation of "cognitive and emotional dissonances" (Wellcome Trust, 2006). This creative process often incorporates the entwining of personal and scientific narratives. To take one example, artists from Stan's Cafe Theatre Company worked with science teachers and young people to create performance installations illustrating the impact of epidemics and vaccination on global populations. The creative educational intervention was the idea to use rice to represent people (one grain = one person). The opportunity for collective, creative participation lay in the young people's decisions on which statistics to use and how to juxtapose them for emotional impact. The science learning lay around developing an understanding of vaccination, research skills, the use of data and evidence. One of the young participants tried to explain the impact:

Left:
Schoolchildren in Stan's Cafe
Theatre Company's Plague
Nation project, funded under the
Wellcome Trust's Pulse scheme.

> Usually you'd see a statistic in numbers and it'd look big and you might think, oh yeah, that's quite a lot of people but when you actually see you think, it's a lot of people, it really sinks in, it really brings out a lot of feeling towards the people there, it's like seeing the people really…when you see the finished mounds of rice and you know that you've weighed it out, so you know it's really accurate then it's really in a way it's unbelievable, you know it's true but you just can't believe it when you actually see it yourself. (Wellcome Trust, 2006, p. 34)

This sense of wonder and the redefinition of the young people's learning spaces is not citizenship in the sense of an individualised exercise of rights or a relationship to a national political entity, but something much closer to citizenship as practical engagement.

If we are to work towards an education that will equip young people as the global scientific citizens or citizen scientists that Rotblat envisioned in order to meet global scientific challenges, it seems we must work together to search for the right interventions entwining a creative approach to science with an equally creative conception of citizenship. As hard as this may sound, in a keynote speech in 2002 on the relevance of science to citizenship education, Rotblat, at that stage into his 90s, was still not downhearted about the potential of educators and others to do this. As he asserted:

> Just as advances in science have made world citizenship an urgent necessity, they have also made it achievable. (Wellcome Trust, 2002)

The practices discussed in this book suggest that it is a task best undertaken by creative educators from all disciplines working together. Whether it is artists working with science teachers, drama teachers working with scientists or young people working with adults, it is the emergence of social solidarities across disciplines and boundaries of all types that gives us some grounds for sharing Rotblat's optimism as well as his vision. What approach to creativity can encapsulate such aspirations?

Encountering creativity

Within recent debates sparked by the resurgence of interest in creativity, it is difficult to find anyone involved in education who advocates uncreative learning. Investigations into creative learning have stressed that creativity flows through all walks of life and all domains of knowledge and, far from remaining the preserve of the arts and humanities, creativity is now regularly associated with the sciences, mathematics, engineering, economics and management. In part, this renewed interest in creativity across the Western world is due to changing economic circumstances in post-industrial societies. The creative industries have become increasingly valued not only for their contribution to cultural life but also for their ability to generate wealth, and a new knowledge-based economy requires employees to be creative, innovative and flexible. With the notable exception of the euphemistic 'creative' accountancy, creativity is widely thought to make a positive contribution to contemporary society, promising a unique combination of personal fulfilment, job satisfaction and economic prosperity. It is unsurprising, therefore, that in a political climate where organisations and industries are relying on creativity for their ability to compete in a global market place, encouraging or 'nurturing' creativity is becoming increasingly central to educational policies and practice.[2]

Whatever the motivations for this renewed interest in creativity may be, and however variously the term is interpreted, explorations into creative learning offer a timely opportunity to reconceptualise the relationship between the arts and sciences. Traditional oppositions between the sciences (objective, factual and impartial) and the arts (subjective, spontaneous and intuitive) seem increasingly redundant, together with stereotypical images of the scientist as a mad, white-coated and bespectacled man and the artist as an eccentric or isolated melancholic. Where such conventional oppositions between the arts and sciences are maintained, it might be expected that collaborations between them would emphasise the role of the arts to exercise a much-needed humanising influence on the arid factuality of science. In this conceptualisation, beauty is the sole preserve of the arts, and the sciences remain remote from the flimsiness of aesthetic judgements and the emotional distractions of empathy. If, however, both the sciences and the arts can make claims to creative thinking and learning, questions might be raised about how learning in the sciences is aided by intuition and moments of insight, and how the processes of working in the arts might make stronger claims for forms of investigation that are rigorous and methodical.

Reconfiguring the relationship between the arts and sciences, and offering ways to think about creative encounters between them, requires reflection on the creative processes that accompany these different modes of practice and contrasting ways of seeing. Creative juxtapositions between the arts and sciences provide young people with the opportunity to question their own ways of learning. Throughout this book it is noticeable that artists and scientists use similar vocabularies to describe their working practices: both talk of experimenting, risk-taking, testing, interpreting, observing and investigating as integral to their methodologies. Furthermore, many contributors comment on the emotional impulses that motivate their work, and how their sense of wonderment and enthusiasm for exploring particular aspects of science has captured the imaginations of young people in collaborative projects with artists.

While the language that is associated with creativity and creative approaches to learning is often associated with the emotions, there is, of course, no guarantee that well-motivated and inspired young people who are actively absorbed in experiments are working creatively. Not only has creativity been theorised from a range of perspectives, including sociology, psychology, education and philosophy; the rhetoric of creativity has been assimilated into policies where its meanings are often vague or oversimplified.[3] Often conflated with individual talent, some theories of creativity have tended to emphasise specific personality traits, or point to particular modes of behaviour. The work of the psychologist Mihaly Csikszentmihalyi offers a good explanation of this way of thinking. In his influential study of creativity, he outlines a generalised theory of creativity, which, while it takes some account of cultural and societal influences, is based on an assessment of personality traits. He describes creative individuals as more complex than 'normal' people because they are able to hold simultaneously apparently paradoxical qualities; he includes realism and imagination, humility and pride as examples of such conflicting impulses (1997, pp. 55–76). He identifies ten "antithetical traits" that he observes in all creative individuals, and his challenge to the dialectic between the arts and sciences is based on this premise: "when a person starts to work creatively...the artist may be as much of a realist as the physicist, and the physicist as imaginative as the artist" (p. 64). According to Csikszentmihalyi, although some personalities have a strong disposition towards creativity, it can be cultivated in the more ordinary activities of everyday life if people are prepared to modify their behaviour by breaking with routine, thereby "liberating" their "creative energies" (p. 344). In such behaviourist conceptualisations of creativity, personal freedom and creativity are assumed to be coterminous and formal education is often thought to stifle originality.

Creativity, according to theoretical models that measure behaviour and personality, has been codified as a five-stage process. It begins with a period of preparation, moves through an incubation phase, insights are then generated (sometimes called the inspirational 'Aha!' moment) after which follows a period of evaluation. The final phase is elaboration, a period during which ideas are translated into tangible forms. While broadly accepting these components, Csikszentmihalyi warns against linearity, arguing that the creative process is often more recursive and circular than this model implies (1997, pp. 79–80). For artists, teachers and scientists involved in developing young people's creativity, this model can provide a helpful way to recognise the different phases the work might undergo, and it can offer ways to structure the learning process. In practical terms, creative learning is likely to be found in classrooms where children are encouraged to combine their subject knowledge with personal experience, and when they are given time to reflect on their learning as well as to generate ideas. Constructing this learning environment requires planning for different phases of the creative process; it suggests that young people's creativity is supported when teachers put structures in place.

The limitation of Csikszentmihalyi's model, however, lies less in its codification of the creative process, and more in the ways it both individualises creativity and assumes that such generalised patterns of creative behaviour can be transferred across all areas of human activity. Those who take risks, think divergently, make connections, ask questions, solve problems and so on are widely regarded as creative, although the relationship between creativity and collaboration has been overlooked or misunderstood. The individualisation of creativity chimes well with a target-driven education system, and it is noticeable that students' achievements are often measured according to specific predetermined indicators.[4] Sometimes young people are asked to evaluate their own creative processes according to criteria that emphasise their private, inner thoughts rather than collaboration and discussion. A good example of this way of thinking about creativity is a framework that is currently promoted by Creative Partnerships' Creativity Wheel, where all statements for children's self-evaluation begin with the word 'I'. Examples include:

> I can create things in my mind.
> I can see more than one way of looking at things.
> I can think of unusual ways of doing things.
> I can see if my work has a purpose.

This emphasis on the first-person pronoun seems to negate the significance of collaboration in the creative classroom. Of course, sometimes creative practice is highly individual, but more often creativity in both the arts and sciences involves a complex process of collaboration, where it is forgotten where the idea came from and unnecessarily competitive to remember who had an idea first.

The collaborations between artists and scientists discussed in this book suggest that individualised models of creativity are ripe for revision. Although educationalists have recognised the importance of domain-specific knowledge and skills to creative processes, one of the recurring themes in accounts of practice discussed in this book is the relationship between innovation, history and society. In their chapter on chimeras and genetic hybrids, Elio Caccavale and Michael Reiss show how collaboration between artists and scientists has the potential to create new domains of knowledge, not only in response to scientific progress, but also as a way of asking moral questions about the future of society. By inviting young people to make decisions, they are able to integrate their knowledge about science with their understanding of the role of the arts. This draws attention to the pace of social change, and recognises that both the arts and sciences are responsive to their contemporary contexts and have the potential to have an impact on the future.

Social psychologist Robert Weisberg argues that creativity is a context-specific process, supported by social networks and cultural geographies. He cites Watson and Crick's discovery of the structure of the DNA molecule as a good example of the impact of situation and setting. Watson and Crick came from different scientific backgrounds, allowing them to see the problem from different perspectives and, Weisberg argues, their methods of working were incremental and collaborative rather than reliant on flashes of inspiration. Watson and Crick were not the only scientists working on DNA in the 1950s and, had the setting and circumstances of their investigations been different, other scientists would have undoubtedly made the discovery. Using this case study as evidence, Weisberg builds his theory of creativity on systems and material conditions rather than on individual personality or patterns of behaviour (1986, pp. 91–98).

It is evident in the partnerships between scientists and artists documented in this book that there is a creative space to be found where experts in both fields work at the edge of their conceptual understanding. Chris Bilton, writing about the management of creativity, argues that creativity flourishes when people from different or divergent perspectives are brought together to investigate a shared problem or question. Bilton recognises the impact of individual spontaneity and insight, but also suggests that the composition of groups or teams is integral to creative learning and thinking. Rather than ascribing roles to individual team members based on psychometric tests, learning styles or different forms of intelligence that are often difficult to break once acquired, he proposes that creativity is based on a flexible balance between specialist expertise and a shared understanding of the problem or brief. "Innovative thinking", Bilton argues, "requires a dialectical process, challenging assumptions from one frame of reference by layering in criticisms from another" (2007, p. 35).

Encounters between scientists and artists are particularly creative when interactions between the two areas of study and practice are allowed to inform and shape each other. The evaluation of the Pulse projects in 2006 provides a good example of how one discipline is altered and reconstructed by its encounter with another:

> The participatory arts were shown both to **facilitate** the communication of science and to **reconstruct** science as a set of open, adventurous, inclusive, alive, enjoyable and dynamic processes, with relevant (inspiring, shocking, emotive) concepts about the world. (Wellcome Trust, 2006, p. 8)

The ability to move productively and dynamically across disciplinary and conceptual limits is facilitated, according to Bilton, by the imposition of constraints and boundaries. Contemporary creativity theory has rejected the idea that freedom from external constraints provides the best conditions for creative collaborations, recognising instead that creativity is as dependent on rule-making as it is on rule-breaking. The argument is summarised by Bilton:

> Creative thinkers understand and acknowledge the context in which they are working, and recognise the constraints imposed by genre, technique and tradition. Having recognised these constraints, they push up against the limits of the possible, testing the boundaries of the field from the inside out. The moment of transformation comes not from thinking outside

the box but from rethinking and redefining the shape of the box from within. (2007, p. 77)

Applied to collaborations between science and the arts, this systemic theory of creativity implies that the synthesis of ideas is dependent on an understanding of differentiated expertise and a willingness to test boundaries and make new rules. This way of thinking about creativity effectively breaks the perception that scientific knowledge is fixed and unerringly authoritative, and promises to both disturb the restrictions of patterns of thought and open new possibilities for meaning-making.

There is no particular obstacle as to why such a way of thinking should not be applied to practice in schools as well as other arenas of arts–science collaborations. From this perspective we can now put certain accepted pedagogical practices under the spotlight. In training for teachers in secondary schools, at least in the one-year courses for graduates, pre-service teachers focus mainly on their subject. There is therefore little opportunity for those new to the teaching profession to engage in interdisciplinary discourses and explore problems together. Yet, in a multidisciplinary science such a narrow focus risks being out of kilter with the contemporary world. In an article on the use of evidence by professionals, Glen Aikenhead (2005) demonstrates how nurses use happiness, emotion, feelings as data sources to make judgements. Thus, they can tell how a patient is responding to treatment by changes in disposition, whether they are happier or more comfortable. The point here is that understanding evidence has broad connotations. In the context of a science lesson it might suggest accuracy and reliability of scientific measuring instruments such as thermometers, for a historian evidence relates to the accuracy of sources from texts, for an RE teacher it might be evidence from a particular ethical position, for an English teacher the way an idea is represented in diverse media. But it is more than this. As the quote from Stan's Cafe so potently shows, it was the impact of the mounds of rice that turned numbers into a sense of social justice. Unless teachers collaborate in an interdisciplinary way it becomes difficult to test those ideas, so prevalent in contemporary science, that extend beyond their own domains.

Creative futures

The present is perhaps best understood through the narratives of history, and in this introduction we have sought to contextualise popular perceptions of sciences and the arts in order to challenge them. Locating abstract thought as well as more material inventions and discoveries within their historical contexts enables us to better imagine the future, or at least to acknowledge what is unimaginable. The arts and the sciences have always upheld established modes of thought as well as providing ways to subvert authority and create social change. It is precisely because there is no guarantee that either mode of inquiry will contribute to creating a just society that education should engage young people in ethical questions about how they will define their roles as citizens.

One of the recurring themes in this book is that we are defined ethically by our interactions with others. This means that finding the creative space that links together the sciences and the arts is inherently a social practice, dependent on children working together and developing mutual understandings. If creative encounters between the arts and sciences are to be both playful and rigorous, they will not dissolve the parameters of each, but they will inspire curiosity by gathering insights from different perspectives. The sciences and the arts, as necessary partners, will create new spaces for wonderment and contexts for questioning and telling stories.

1 WHO, 2006, Annex Table 1.

2 The phrase 'nurturing creativity' is used by a Department for Culture, Media and Sport report written by Paul Roberts (2006) to inform policy on creativity and young people. The phrase implies that creativity is innate, and underlines the significance of preparing young people to participate in a creative economy.

3 See Banaji and Burn (2006).

4 An example of this way of thinking about creative individuals in education might be found in the Qualifications and Curriculum Authority document, *Creativity: Find it, promote it* (2003) that defines four characteristics of creativity.

Bibliography

Aikenhead G. Science-based occupations and the science curriculum: concepts of evidence. Science Education 2005;89(2):242–75.

Banaji S, Burn A. The Rhetorics of Creativity: A review of the literature. London: Arts Council England; 2006.

Bilton C. Management and Creativity. Oxford: Basil Blackwell; 2007.

Csikszentmihalyi M. Creativity: Flow and the psychology of discovery and invention. New York: Harper Collins; 1997.

Layton D, Jenkins E, Macgill S, Davey, A. Inarticulate science? Driffield: Studies in Education Ltd; 1993.

Leach M, Scoones I, Wynne B. Science and Citizens. London: Zed; 2005.

Marshall TH. Citizenship and Social Class. Cambridge: CUP; 1950.

Michael M, Brown N. Scientific citizenships: self-representations of xenotransplantation's publics. Science as Culture 2005;14(1):39–57.

Nowotny H, Scott P, Gibbons M. Re-thinking Science: Knowledge and the public in the age of uncertainty. Cambridge: Polity Press; 2001.

Qualifications and Curriculum Authority. Creativity: Find it, promote it. London: DfES; 2003. www.ncaction.org.uk/creativity.

Roach J. The Player's Passion: Studies in the science of acting. Ann Arbor: University of Michigan Press; 1993.

Roberts P. Nurturing Creativity: A report to government to inform future policy. London: DCMS; 2006.

Rotblat J. Nobel Prize Acceptance Speech. Nobel Foundation; 1995. www.pugwash.org/award/Rotblatnobel.htm.

Weisberg RW. Creativity: Genuis and other myths. New York: W.H. Freeman and Company; 1986.

Wellcome Trust. Science and Citizenship: A step forward. London: Wellcome Trust; 2002.

Wellcome Trust. Making it Live: An evaluation of Pulse (phase 1). London: Wellcome Trust; 2006.

World Health Organization. The World Health Report 2006 – Working together for health. Geneva: WHO; 2006. www.who.int/whr/2006/en/index.html.

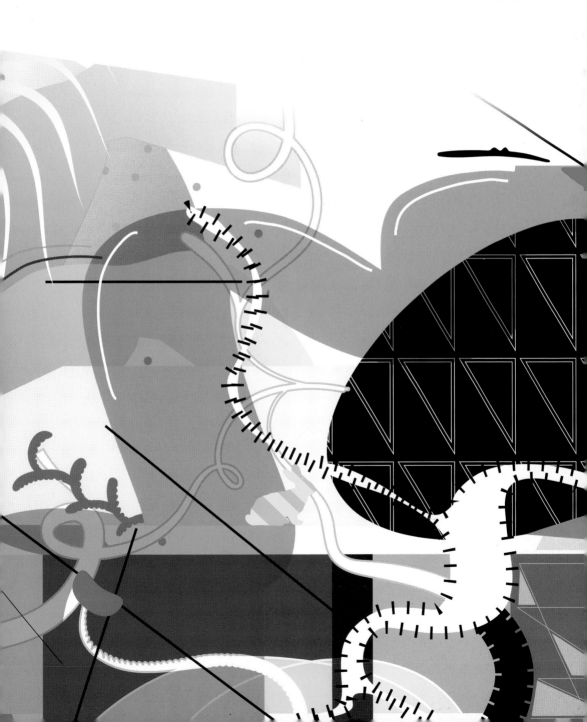

Introducing wonder

Helen Nicholson

This section assesses the experience of wonder in young people's education. Wonder is, in many ways, a problematic term to apply to education; the word is more often associated with miracles and magic, with suspiciously supernatural and mystical practices rather than with the more everyday classroom reality of rigorous and measurable educational objectives.

Asking teachers to encourage 'awe and wonder' in their classrooms as was once advocated by the National Curriculum in England seemed unreasonably idealistic, leaving teachers to question whether its authors had actually faced any restless classes on a wet afternoon. Yet away from the suspicions of mysticism and the more burdensome trials of teaching, the experience of wonder remains a potent element in learning. This section seeks to redefine the relationship between the arts and sciences in education through reconceptualising the idea of wonder.

One of the risks in suggesting that encouraging wonder is an important aspect of learning is that it conjures up images of public demonstrations of scientific experiments that are perhaps heavier on performance than substance. There is a long tradition of public engagement with science through entertainment, not all of which has been designed to offer insights into scientific thought. The 19th-century inventor Thomas Edison, for example, was renowned for promoting his phonograph through performances in which he would conduct conversations with the machine. The sense of wonder that Edison's performances inspired, however, were used to promote consumerist desire rather than to offer technical information. The seductive spectacle of Edison's scientific invention was offered for public amazement, setting Edison apart as one of the first capitalist scientists (Case, 2007, p. 80). Although there are many examples of scientists who have used the medium of performance to encourage public engagement, this legacy has led to the perception that the sense of wonder promoted by performance is more likely to mystify and astonish rather than promote knowledge and understanding.

So how might wonder be rescued from the flimsiness of seduction and applied to the more robust elements of education? One answer might be to examine the aesthetic qualities of science, both intrinsic to science itself and made visible in the interpretation of scientific concepts and ideas in artistic form. The association between the arts, sciences and mathematics is long and enduring; the abstract work of sculptors Henry Moore and Barbara Hepworth, for example, was directly influenced by their contemporaries studying geometry. More recently, in 2007, the artist and designer Helen Storey's collaboration with the physical chemist Tony Ryan, director of the Polymer Centre at the University of Sheffield, has had both scientific and artistic benefits. Motivated by a mutual interest in environmental issues, the collaboration has led to new materials made from polymers that can dissolve. Disappearing bottles, which can be dissolved in hot water, are among the patented products resulting from this collaboration that form part of an exhibition. Displayed alongside these more functional inventions are Helen Storey's explorations of the artistic and aesthetic qualities of the new material, and her dissolving dresses are a central focus of this meeting of laboratory and the studio in the gallery. This project is appropriately entitled 'Wonderland'.[1]

Applied to young people's learning, as drama educationalist Joe Winston points out in this section, a sense of wonderment is allied to the experience of beauty. The beautiful has been associated with feelings of connectivity and pleasure, and has also inspired moral debate about the relationship between beauty and truth. Drawing on the philosophical work of Alexander Nehamas and the aesthetic pedagogy of Mark Girod, Winston makes a persuasive case for the place of beauty in education, both as qualities intrinsic to mathematics and science and as a powerful means of inspiring young people to learn.

Winston's exploration of the pedagogic power of beauty draws attention to the poetics of science, and this is another way to look at the relationship between the arts and sciences in education. Science and mathematics depend on the poetic for their explanations; scientific concepts are frequently reliant on metaphor to communicate ideas and mathematics is rich in abstract symbolism. This is well recognised in literary interpretations of scientific and mathematical concepts; Alice's Wonderland was, famously, a metaphor for the absurdities of life as lived by Oxford's eccentric scientists and mathematicians. Rich in mathematical references, the novel reveals that life, when stripped of illusion, becomes a tale of nonsense. In their work on illusion and perception, neuroscientist Beau Lotto and neuropsychologist Richard Gregory worked with the story of *Through the Looking-glass* to create an exhibition that invited young and not-so-young visitors to explore how their brains perceive visual images.[2] In his chapter in this section, Beau Lotto extends his discussion of the significance of illusion in education. By working alongside the visual artist Sara Downham and head teacher David Strudwick, Lotto suggests how five- and six-year-old children can learn to recognise how they perceive patterns, shapes and illusions in their everyday lives. Through this work, Lotto argues, children's interest is stimulated in the world around them – encouraging them to be, as Alice might have said, 'curiouser and curiouser'. This curiosity is not only a prerequisite for good science education; Lotto and his collaborators also suggest that illusion is a metaphor for education, and exploring perception enables children to see things empathetically from different perspectives and points of view.

If beauty and illusion are significant to science and arts education, their perceived opposites, the monstrous and the grotesque, also attract young people's interest. This interest signals another way to apply wonder to science education; there is an enduring fascination with gothic novels and horror films that test the limits of the possible and the moral that appeal to young people. The artist Elio

Caccavale and science educationalist Michael Reiss have investigated students' interest in the grotesque and miraculous by focusing on chimeras and genetic hybrids. Their work illustrates the importance of raising ethical questions with young people about the effects of scientific developments, especially where nature is modified through new biotechnologies. In this context, the products of the scientific imagination inspire strong emotional responses, not only of wonder and amazement at scientific innovation, but also of repulsion and disturbance to what appears grotesque and unnatural.

Taken together, the authors collected in this section share an interest in the ways in which the pedagogic power of wonder can be integrated into collaborations between artists and scientists in education. Science, like the arts, has aesthetic and poetic qualities, and the authors represented here concur that the senses of curiosity, shock, empathy, pleasure and disgust are all part of the passion of learning. Wonder is, etymologically, an Old English word that has long been allied to the positive qualities of admiration and achievement as well as having more negative associations with a sense of horror and destruction. This is the vocabulary of creativity, ethics and moral debate and, as such, deserves a place in the education of young citizens.

1 www.helenstoreyfoundation.org/wonderland/1.htm.
2 This was developed in partnership with At-Bristol, and toured nationally. www.at-bristol.org.uk/explore/alice.htm.

Bibliography
Case S-E. Performing Science and the Virtual. London: Routledge; 2007.

Mathematics, science and the liberating beauty of theatre

Joe Winston

Beauty is a concept more usually associated with the arts than the sciences. Yet many scientists and mathematicians perceive beauty in the phenomena they study. This beauty, notes *Joe Winston*, is not an aesthetic judgement but a deep emotional and inspirational experience. Among other things, it can inspire learning. Incorporating this experience into the teaching and testing routines of modern science education is not straightforward, yet failing to acknowledge the importance of beauty threatens to marginalise an experience that should be central to children's learning.

Introduction

It is nothing controversial to argue that current educational thinking, in policy and practice, is dominated by the languages of target-setting, performance management, skills acquisition and quantifiable assessment criteria. Behind this lies a belief that only what can be measured, or demonstrated clearly, or backed up by facts can be trusted; and in an age of increasing global economic competitiveness, certainties about increased performance and rising standards are seen as necessary in order to ensure future prosperity. The resultant rhetoric – of improvement, efficiency gains and best practice – may well, as Onora O'Neill has argued, sound admirable enough but beneath it "the real focus is on performance indicators chosen for ease of measurement and control rather than because they measure quality of performance accurately". (2002, p. 54). The danger, then, is that those more elusive qualities that education may legitimately concern itself with can become sidelined or ignored. In such a climate, it is small wonder that the concept of beauty should be relatively unheard-of in educational discourse, especially within the disciplines of maths and science. Despite the fact that statements about the uncertainty of science can be found in most national examination specifications in the UK, there is still a 'common-sense' view among teachers, influenced by the dominant educational ideology, that these subjects deal in the kind of certainties best suited to clear and transparent objectives-based teaching. This chapter will, however, propose that the more elusive qualities of beauty have a place in their teaching; and that to ignore this is to fail to appreciate the power of beauty to motivate a desire to learn.

Above:
Scene from *A Disappearing Number*.

Joris-Jan Bos

Learning from *A Disappearing Number*

Numbers are pervasively significant in the contemporary world. Through clocks, mobile phones, prices, weights, bus and train timetables, TV and radio channels, account numbers, paycheques, they regulate and order our daily lives. In schools they provide the quantitative data of test scores and percentiles used to measure attainment and verify accountability. The power and nature of numbers was, however, explored very differently in a recent play, *A Disappearing Number*, conceived and directed by Simon McBurney and performed by Theatre Complicité.[1] The piece was experimental in form, crossing time and space, telling parallel and interrelated stories that centred upon the lives of two mathematicians. One of these is Srinivasa Ramanujan, the mathematical genius, who moved from a job in a clerk's office in India to work at Cambridge University during World War I, before dying tragically young. A similar untimely death befalls the fictional character, Sarah, a university lecturer, whose research focus is the work of Ramanujan. The principal character, however, is very much a non-mathematician called Alex. The play opens in the form of a maths lecture, where Sarah introduces the formula of a complex equation developed by Ramanujan, whose proposition $(1 + 2 + 3 + 4 \ldots \infty = -\frac{1}{2})$ seems incomprehensible, absurd even, to the average member of the audience. This is also where Alex meets her for the first time, starting a process for him that begins as a love affair but becomes a quest for understanding; for the more he grows to love Sarah, the more he needs to understand what it is that drives her passion for her subject. Their story is told episodically, and Sarah's fascination parallels that of the historical figure G H Hardy,

Theatre is an ephemeral art form, the most impermanent of all, like our lives, existing only in space and time.

author of *A Mathematician's Apology*, who invited Ramanujan to lecture in Cambridge. If the progression of the play finds its dynamic in both Alex's and Sarah's quests for understanding, its artfulness stems from McBurney's parallel fascination with the mysterious power of numbers and his attempt to realise in theatrical form the beauty of the mathematical concepts that connect the characters' lives. A hint to this is provided on a photograph in the programme notes. McBurney is shown in front of a blackboard, at the centre of which he has written the word 'beauty'. Along a horizontal axis, this is connected to a mathematical equation through the words 'constancy', 'performance', 'certainty'; the vertical axis sees it connected to the human world, which includes the words 'uncertainty' and 'imagination', and also 'theatre'.

The play engages these two ideas of beauty – the ideal and the material – in a dance between the mathematical concepts at its core and the aesthetics of theatre that give them expression. Key among these is the theory that everything is interconnected through time and space through numbers, an idea that goes back at least as far as Pythagoras and has resurfaced more recently as an element of string theory.[2] One of the play's key symbols is patterned through the classical Indian music and dance that permeate its formal structure, relating Ramanujan and a series of minor characters to their cultural roots through an art form that depends heavily on vocal rhythmic counting, rooting art and number to a sense of cultural and historical tradition. Around this illusion of constancy, the material reality of the stage space is continually and visibly transformed to denote shifts in time, as in a scene that begins with Sarah delivering a lecture on Ramanujan's work. While she does this, we see the actor playing the part of Hardy take up a position directly behind her. As she quotes from a lecture he gave in the 1920s, he begins to speak with her, then continues the lecture on his own, relocating the audience in historical time as the actor playing Sarah leaves the stage.

Crispin Sartwell has suggested that beauty matters so much to us because it captures our longing for permanence; in his words: "Beauty is the string of connection between a finite creature and a time-bound world" (2004, p. 150). This tension between the finite and the infinite is encapsulated neatly in two scenes; once through a discussion of what is often referred to as Zeno's second paradox – that $1 + \frac{1}{2} + \frac{1}{4} + \frac{1}{8} + \frac{1}{16} + \frac{1}{32}$ etc. will eventually make two but only an infinite two[3] – then in the final scene, where Alex visits Sarah's grave. There he holds a piece of chalk, found in her trunk, identical to the chalk she held when he first met her, the chalk with which she wrote the mathematical equations that left her trace on the world. As he stands there, ashes and sand – or is it powdered chalk? – begin to pour over the stage, an image of death and of time running out. This is accompanied by the sound of a number pattern being repeated and repeated, gradually fading. Theatre is an ephemeral art form, the most impermanent of all, like our lives, existing only in space and time. When the chalk/sand/ashes cease to fall, the lights dim and the play is over; but the numbers keep repeating, ever fainter yet still distinct; for a while at least, through the illusion of theatre, it seems that they will continue to be repeated infinitely.

What I have called somewhat grandly "the liberating beauty of theatre" could equally be called in this instance "the liberating beauty of mathematics", capturing as it does a personal response to this particular play. *A Disappearing Number* reminded me that numbers need not only be used to quantify, order and control our lives but that they are also mysterious and fascinating. The truths they promise can be elusive, paradoxical and play tricks on our human rationality. Above all, they can be sources of wonder and this is at the heart of what John Armstrong (2005) has called "the secret power of beauty".

Learning through beauty in science education

> For some people the contemplation of scientific theories is an experience hardly less golden than the experience of being in love or looking at a sunset. (Haldane, cited in Mark Girod, 2006, p. 47)

Beauty is not something we need to look up in a dictionary to understand. It is a word common to all of us and, although we may not all find the same things beautiful, we understand each other quite readily enough when we use the word. The philosophers of ancient Greece were very clear about beauty, what it meant and how central it was as a human value. Aristotle postulated that to find something beautiful was to find in it a quality of excellence that kindled an emotion akin to love; we can locate this meaning in common usage today when people talk about a beautiful tune, a beautiful dress, a beautiful smile. Plato had a lot to say about beauty, too, some of which might be less evident to modern sensibilities. In works such as *Phaedrus* and the *Symposium* he constructed an argument that linked it essentially with *eros* – with pleasure, passion and desire – in which the longing inspired by beauty was intimately connected to a longing for goodness and truth. As Nehamas explains, for Plato:

> ...all beautiful things draw us beyond themselves, leading us to recognize and love other, more precious beauties, culminating in the love of beauty itself and the happy life of philosophy. (2007, p. 6)

Even at its highest, most idealised form, however, "beauty cannot be sundered from understanding or desire. The most abstract and intellectual beauty provokes the urge to possess it no less than the most sensual inspires the passion to come to know it better" (ibid., p. 7). This account of the cognitive energy of beauty is very much in line with Alex's experience in *A Disappearing Number*. He begins by desiring Sarah, in whom he finds beauty, just as we find beauty in anyone we love. But his desire does not stop with possessing her physically. He wishes to understand her, which means he wishes to understand what she understands, appreciate what she loves.

> Beautiful things direct our attention to everything else we must learn and acquire to understand and possess them and they quicken the sense of life, giving it new sense and direction. (ibid., p. 76)

In the play, Alex remains perplexed, as he lacks the mathematical grounding to begin to make sense of the complexity of it all. But along the way he learns and makes inroads, as we do, and at least comes to understand how and why Sarah is in thrall to mathematics: not because of its potential applications or its practical uses but because of its beauty. As Dirac once famously said: "It is more important to have beauty in one's equations than to have them fit the experiment" (cited in Girod, p. 40). This is what provides her learning with its future-oriented dynamic, what drives her to want to understand more. Nothing is ever settled and her desire to carry on learning, to know better, continues. This passionate quest to learn inspired by beauty is summed up in the words of Elaine Scarry:

> The beautiful, almost without any effort of our own, acquaints us with the mental event of conviction, and so pleasurable a mental state is this, that ever afterwards one is willing to labor, struggle, wrestle with the world to locate enduring sources of conviction – to locate what is true. (2001, p. 31)

Small wonder that she goes on to state that "beauty is a starting place for education". But such a starting place has little in common with the currently dominant objectives-based approach that concentrates on quantifying and measuring whether something has been learned or not. This does not energise a desire or longing to learn, a point wryly made by the following true story:

If we relate the objectives approach directly to science, we can see that its technicism ignores the deeper mysteries and wonders that have inspired the many genuine scientists with a passion for their subject.

An eight-year-old boy…was asked 'Do you think you ought to learn to read?' Having answered in the affirmative, he was then asked, 'Why do you think you should?' to which the reply was 'Then I can stop', a response that might have been thought of, even though not expressed, by many less honest pupils! (Arnold, 1982, p. 16)

Achievable objectives do of course have their place in education and there are those elements of learning that are factual and necessary that can be usefully and visibly assessed. But these are small steps inside a much wider context. They are not in themselves purposeful and attaining them does not generate satisfaction for the learner beyond any immediate sense of mastery. If we relate the objectives approach directly to science, we can see that its technicism ignores the deeper mysteries and wonders that have inspired the many genuine scientists with a passion for their subject, a desire to make sense of what they do not yet understand. As Girod has pointed out:

> Often in the retelling of a scientific discovery the 'human', 'creative', 'inspired' and 'passionate' sides of scientists and their stories get left out. These are often deemed unimportant or anti-intellectual, pulling readers away from the important details of theory development, research results and solutions to equations. (2006, p. 39)

This omission is due to a pervasive belief that science, like maths, is a world of paradigms, models and laws, of pure reason, above and beyond the human world of narrative and metaphor, art and emotion. Yet maths and science are alive with symbols and, as Kuhn has taught us, have their own historical narratives within which they locate their arguments and develop their theories. And these, as the quotation from Dirac above reminds us, are guided by the human delight in beauty as well as truth. "It was aesthetics and not observation that refuted Ptolemy and led to Copernicus"

(Sartwell, 2004, p. 20) – Sartwell's claim is provocatively partial but his point is nonetheless profound. Ptolemy's cosmology may well have accounted for what astronomers were able to observe, but its narrative of cycles, epicycles and epiepicycles lacked the simple elegance of Copernicus's heliocentric explanation for the same observations.

In Girod's recent work on the place of beauty in science and in science education, he is much influenced by John Dewey. As Nehamas recognises with the Platonic tradition of beauty, so Girod recognises with Dewey's account of aesthetic experience – that Dewey reintroduces this experience into the common language of the everyday, democratising it as a condition of living in the world rather than as something pertaining only to art houses and museums. Girod usefully summarises what Dewey sees as the conditions characteristic of having an experience as distinct from the common flow of experience typical of everyday living:

> An experience is contrasted with ordinary experience and is identified as having a series of qualities including (1) the fusing or intermingling of thought, emotion and action; (2) the expansion of one's perception literally creating new ways of seeing the world, and; (3) an increased feeling of value for this newfound perspective. The process of having *an* experience typically unfolds through a transaction between the person and world in which each emerges as different than before the experience. (2006, p. 48)

This definition helps us see that beauty's role in science education can best be grasped in terms of the experiences it can provide, rather than through the targets and outcomes that science in schools has all too often been reduced to. It also presents beauty's energies as cognitive as well as sensory, and transformative rather than cumulative. In other words, an apprehension of beauty can change students' perceptions dramatically, allowing them to grasp

All of these activities can help children wonder at the beauty of colour and light and, by sharing in their curiosity and excitement, teachers can help lay a foundation for the conceptual knowledge that later years can build upon.

the error or ignorance of their previous, common-sense understandings. I am not suggesting that teachers who work within the framework of the National Curriculum cannot provide learning experiences of this kind but that it requires a vision that looks beyond the prescribed learning outcomes.

"Science is replete with powerful ideas that have the potential to lead us into Deweyian experiences if we are open to them and allow them to unfold," writes Girod (p. 50). This is a comment interestingly reminiscent of the words of the art critic, Michael Kimmelman, who wrote about beauty being "out there waiting to be captured, the only question being whether we are prepared to recognize it" (2005, p. 5) and is something that foundation-stage/early-years teachers can readily convey to their pupils in topics such as light and colour. Children can investigate prisms and then create their own by pouring oil on top of a plate of water; they can shine torches on mirrors or through coloured gels in a 'dark cave' created by blacking out the home corner; they can mix colours with powder paint; make their own spinning circles to see how colours merge to create new colours; and make simple kaleidoscopes from card, plastic mirrors and coloured beads. All of these activities can help children wonder at the beauty of colour and light and, by sharing in their curiosity and excitement, teachers can help lay a foundation for the conceptual knowledge that later years can build upon.

Pugh and Girod outline a pedagogy, based on their own research, intended to move towards what they call a "transformative, aesthetic science education". The principles that underlie this are listed below (2007, p.14) with my own summaries of their lengthy explanations in italics:

Methods of crafting ideas out of concepts
(ideas about how to transform ordinary concepts into
compelling ideas that will lead students to see and experience
the world in a new way)

- Restore concepts to the experience in which they had their
  origin and significance: *help students understand the power these
  concepts had when first discovered by placing them in a clear
  historical context.*
- Foster anticipation and a vital, personal experiencing:
  *treat the lesson as a dramatist would treat a plot, choosing the
  elements of content that are most vital and crafting them together to
  create maximum anticipation and personal involvement.*
- Use metaphors and re-seeing to expand perception:
  *helping us see things anew by breaking routine, making us see the
  commonplace afresh or making the extraordinary apprehensible.*

**Modelling and scaffolding a transformative,
aesthetic experience**
(ideas of how to enculturate students into ways of valuing
and experiencing science ideas)

- Model a passion for the content: *the teacher fosters and
  demonstrates their passion for science.*
- Scaffolding students' action, perception and valuing:
  *help students into deeper levels of understanding by providing
  experiences that move them, for example, from a peripheral to
  a more central participation.*

The sample of activities on light and colour outlined above provide
ready opportunities for teachers to model passion and scaffold
learning in the manner proposed in the final two points. If we turn
our attention to older learners, Clive Sutton gives some excellent
examples of how scientists responsible for major discoveries had to
struggle with language and find the right metaphors in order to
help others enter imaginatively into their new ways of seeing (1992,
p. 41). Harvey's choice of the metaphor of a pump for the heart, for

example, or Robert Hooke's use of the word 'cell' to describe the millions of little cavities he saw in a slice of cork placed under a microscope: both are examples of scientific language arising from excitement and amazement, guided by aesthetic and interpretive choices to capture meaning in language that has since become conventional. A good example provided by Sutton as to how children might recapture this sense of wonder through metaphor relates to Torricelli's realisation in the 19th century that the atmosphere we live in is essentially an "ocean of air". By being introduced to a passage written in 1878 by Arabella Buckley, children can be invited to imagine a being "whose eyes are so made that he could see gases as we see liquids" and to respond to what they imagine this being would see (Sutton, ibid., p. 41).

An example of a lesson planned as an unfolding story, as a dramatic plot guided by the teacher, is provided in a scheme for Key Stage 2 teachers by Linda Atherton, primary science adviser for Warwickshire Educational Development Services. Entering the classroom, the children find their desks moved back and the outline of a corpse chalked on the floor. They are informed by the teacher (in role as a forensic scientist) that there has been a murder for which there are four suspects, whose details are provided on a worksheet. There are also various pieces of evidence near the body, including samples of fabric, powder and a muddy footprint. Children search for clues in order to correlate data already collected and are then asked to interrogate the evidence, make links and detect patterns in a systematic, safe and fair way as it will be presented to a prosecution lawyer to see if there is enough of it to take to court. This is where the activity explores key scientific processes and ideas. Filtering, for example, is a technique that now has a real purpose in order to identify the soils; the white powder samples react in very different ways and allow for discussion of reversible and irreversible reactions; looking at fibres under a digital microscope, the children explore the differences between those that are natural and those man-made. Once children realise the relationship between size of feet and height, they can confidently use this information to predict the height of someone at the scene. Group talk becomes clearly focused on scientific principles and tables are produced to collate evidence. Children have a strong desire to ensure that their methodology is fair and thorough and, of course, an 'expert' is on hand to support the scientific thinking and processes. The courtroom is then set up with the teacher in a new role as prosecutor, asking tough questions about whether and to what extent the evidence incriminates any of the suspects, thus forcing children to re-evaluate what exactly it is telling them and how valid their interpretations have been.

This model of lesson planning approaches the aesthetic experience of theatre and I would like to conclude by looking at two theatrical productions, conceived and developed for children of five years of age and under, one of which was funded by the Wellcome Trust. In doing this, we can examine how mathematical and scientific ideas and applications can be introduced to stimulate very young children's imaginations and cognition through the means of theatre and the power of beauty, to leave them not with any definable learning objectives but something more elusive yet more potent – a sense of fascination and wonder.

Young children experiencing science and beauty through theatre

Theatre-Rites is commonly regarded as one of the foremost and certainly one of the most innovative children's theatre companies currently operating in the UK, specialising in work for audiences of young schoolchildren and pre-school children with their parents. Their performances are characterised by their highly visual quality and their use of multimedia technology to create work that I would describe as playful, striking, exhilarating and beautiful.

The Thought that Counts, which toured in 2007, deals with a range of scientific, mathematical and social issues by exploring the beauty

Above:
Scenes from *Hospitalworks*,
co-produced with Polka Theatre
and Theater der Welt.

Paul Tanner

of the art form and ways it can fashion abstract concepts into memorable theatrical images. Its priority is to provide children with a striking aesthetic experience and, in doing this, it plays with the mathematical concepts of number and ordering, circles and spheres, volume, size and sequencing, with the scientific concepts of gravity and the solar system, and with social ideas such as friendship, separation, loneliness and togetherness. These are playfully realised with strong uses of coloured lighting, sound, music and multimedia, revealing the theatre as a place where anything can be created and explored. The aim is to inspire wonder and leave the children with plenty for their imaginations to dwell upon after the show has concluded. Such work, too, has a moral purpose: in the words of Roger Deldime, the French writer on theatre for children, *"c'est un porteur d'utopies, [qui] suggère que la vie peut et doit être changée, que l'impossible est possible"*[4] (1999, p. 16).

Theatre-Rites's plays do not have a storyline as such but develop through a succession of scenes and images that progress logically from one to the other, principally through the narrative possibilities presented by their visual imagery. In *The Thought that Counts*, the images centred upon five actors, contrasting circles of light and a series of inflatable balloons, or spheres, of differing sizes. At different times these were thought bubbles held over one actor's head as he worried about speaking in public, carriers of different numbers projected on to them, balloons and balls that could be used to play games that would include or exclude different actors, balls that could be bounced on sequences of numbers that appeared and disappeared in a circle of light, planets of the solar system rotated through the darkened space by the actors themselves, or a meteor charging at the surface of the moon. There was also a white, plastic puppet that appeared to self-inflate early on in the performance. During the central, rhythmically slower part of the play, the action focused upon her, as the stage darkened and transformed into a moonscape projected on to the floor. Music and actors all added to the spacewalk effect as they danced slowly over the surface, taking turns to guide the balloon creature and protect her from the attacking meteor. Such playful affects are not designed to teach children how to add up or explain how gravity or the solar system works, of course, but to help, in Sutton's terms, "develop their seeing ability" (1992, p. 40). The aesthetic charm and heightened sensory environment serve to anchor children's attention so that, hopefully, they will leave the theatre fascinated with what they have seen, with memories of planets as spherical objects moving slowly in circles around a larger sphere, and with a sense that walking on one of these worlds is not the same as walking on this one. Such wondering can form the foundations for scientific curiosity.

Above:
Scene from *The Thought that Counts*.
Robert Workman

In *The Thought that Counts*, children are drawn into an awe-inspiring journey through the solar system, where actors walk on the moon and, through the effects of multimedia technology, seem to disappear into giant spheres, sent spinning like space capsules through the darkness. Yet this is done with gentleness and humour and comes between the more domestic charm of scenes where actors play games with one another, where a fragile balloon person self-inflates and children are given their own balloons at the end of the performance as a delicate reminder of the journey they have been on together.

Theatre-Rites worked with Polka Theatre, another London-based company, funded by the Wellcome Trust, to produce a site-specific piece entitled *Hospitalworks* in 2005 and this, too, brought the lighter qualities of beauty – its charm and lively gaiety – into a location normally known for more overwhelming associations of life and death. The event took place in a disused ward of the Mayday University Hospital in Croydon. The audience were led through some of the working parts of the hospital before reaching the performance space, which took the form of a magical ward, where the audience took on the role of visitors and the performers the role of staff in a hospital where the patients were, in fact, the everyday objects in the ward – beds, pillows, lamps. Staff performed the kind of routines of care that one would expect; to this extent, children could observe and learn what these routines consisted of. What made them memorable was the surprisingly playful ways in which they were enacted.[5] So, for example, a bed was examined and diagnosed as having a bad chest; a reluctant pillow puppet was given an injection; children were given sticking plasters to stick over cracks in a wall to help it get better; and they watched nurses assist as a bed gave birth to a pillow. Amid all of these essentially comic elements were woven moments of tenderness and moments of striking visual beauty. At one point, death was represented by a bed covered in colourful flowers being led slowly and silently through the ward. This contrasted with a scene where the newborn pillow was gently cradled and comforted with a lullaby. Part of the show consisted of a less structured, more interactive 'free-play' area where lighting and sound created atmospheric and colourful areas where children could listen with stethoscopes to a (mechanically) 'breathing' bed, be guided through a maze of drip bags hanging from the ceiling and bathed in multicoloured lighting, and use UV torches in an X-ray room to examine the skeletal structure of a hospital bed.

The work of Theatre-Rites is nothing if not openly and powerfully playful, and lest we dismiss play as relevant only to young children, we need to remember how it is not only at the core of theatre making but also, according to the philosopher Friedrich Schiller, both an essential human need and the spur to our creation and appreciation of beauty. He believed that humanity has two basic, conflicting drives, those of sense and of reason. In denying either one superiority over the other, he proposed that a third drive – that of play – served, as something that we naturally enjoy, to keep both reason and sense in their rightful place. The object of play for Schiller is to unite in balance our desire for sensation with our desire for order; and the highest form that this can take, he believed, is in the form of beauty itself.[6] In both of these performance projects, *The Thought that Counts* and *Hospitalworks*, we can see this dance between order and sensation at the heart of their aesthetic; the ordered world of number, of the planetary system, of the applied science and routines of the hospital are playfully explored, disturbed and re-imagined within the heightened sensory environment of the theatrical spaces they created.

Conclusion

There are volumes of complex and difficult literature on beauty and aesthetic philosophy that I have largely avoided in this chapter, wishing to emphasise the immediacy of beauty, the instinctive pull it exerts upon us and those qualities capable of inspiring and motivating us to learn. Beauty is something that both adults and children can talk about and relate to readily and with pleasure. But, of course, we do find different things beautiful. As Kant put it: "there can be no rule by which someone could be compelled to acknowledge that something is beautiful" (1987, p. 59). Although we can argue with some conviction that beauty itself is a universal human value, taste – what we actually find as beautiful – will vary according to culture, age, class, gender, the times we live in and a whole range of determinants that shape individual identities. Theatre, however, is a social event and theatre as joyful and celebratory as the two children's performances described here do, as Colin Counsell has argued, create a forceful draw towards consensus and conformity of response. In his words: "Theatre... provides a mechanism for group discipline and unified interpretation whose efficacy outstrips that of any other artform" (1996, p. 22). Actors perceive the audience just as the audience

The real value of such
projects, I would argue,
is what they teach us about
the power of beauty to
stimulate wonder in
subjects whose disciplines
of knowledge are often
mistakenly blurred with
the reductive agenda of
skills-based learning.

perceives the actors, and in response can subtly modify and adapt their performance. In other words, the experience of beauty through theatre can become shared and powerfully communal. Some hint that this was indeed the case can be found, paradoxically perhaps, through the very quantifiable evaluatory procedures that are nowadays demanded as proof of educational value. Feedback from both family and school audiences for Hospitalworks showed that 65 per cent rated the show as excellent and 28 per cent as very good (beautiful not being one of the categories, of course). Such figures are doubtless heartening, particularly if they lead to further projects of this kind. But the real value of such projects, I would argue, is what they teach us about the power of beauty to stimulate wonder in subjects whose disciplines of knowledge are often mistakenly blurred with the reductive agenda of skills-based learning. Such an argument does, however, present a challenge to educationalists who specialise in theatre as much as those who specialise in science or mathematics. Despite the unavoidable demands to clarify learning objectives and quantify evaluatory procedures, there is a need to remain healthily sceptical of their limitations and not to be seduced by their false certainties. There can be nothing certain or resolved in any attempt to fashion or shape a beautiful experience, but to do so is a core purpose of art; both science and mathematics, to paraphrase the previous quote taken from Pugh and Girod, are replete with ideas and concepts that lend themselves to this purpose.

1 The play was performed at the Warwick Arts Centre at the end of April 2007.

2 See Aristotle's *Metaphysics* and http://superstringtheory.com.

3 See the essay 'Avatars of the Tortoise' in Borges (1970).

4 'it's a bringer of utopias, suggesting that life can and ought to be changed, that the impossible is possible' (my translation).

5 See Deldime and Pigeon (1988) to find support for this statement. The largest quantitative survey to date of the memories of young spectators discovered that surprising visual spectacle remained for longest in their minds.

6 For play as the basis of theatre see Schechner (2002), chapter 4; for a summary of Schiller's theory of beauty see Armstrong (2000), pp. 151–68.

Bilbiography

Armstrong J. The Intimate Philosophy of Art. London: Penguin; 2000.

Armstrong J. The Secret Power of Beauty. London: Penguin; 2005.

Arnold H. Listening to Children Reading. Sevenoaks: Hodder and Stoughton; 1982.

Borges JL. Labyrinths. Harmondsworth: Penguin; 1970.

Counsell C. Signs of Performance: An introduction to twentieth century theatre. London: Routledge; 1996.

Deldime R. Questions de Théâtre 6: D'une rive a l'autre. Brussels: Lansman; 1999.

Deldime R, Pigeon J. La Mémoire du Jeune Spectateur. Brussels: De Boeck; 1988.

Girod M. A conceptual overview of the role of beauty and aesthetics in science and science education. Studies in Science Education 2006;43:38–61.

Kant I. Critique of Judgment. Cambridge: Hackett; 1987 (transl. WS Pluhar).

Kimmelman M. The Accidental Masterpiece: On the art of life and vice-versa. New York: The Penguin Press; 2005.

Nehamas A. Only a Promise of Happiness: The place of Beauty in a world of Art. Princeton: Princeton University Press; 2007.

O'Neill O. A Question of Trust: The BBC Reith Lectures, 2002. Cambridge: Cambridge University Press; 2002.

Pugh K, Girod M. Science, art and experience: constructing a science pedagogy from Dewey's aesthetics. Journal of Science Teacher Education 2007:18(1);9–27.

Sartwell C. Six Names of Beauty. London: Routledge; 2004.

Scarry E. On Beauty and Being Just. London: Duckbacks; 2001.

Schechner R. Performance Studies: An introduction. London: Routledge; 2002.

Sutton C. Words, Science and Learning. Buckingham: Open University Press; 1992.

Winston J. Beauty, goodness and education: the Arts beyond utility. Journal of Moral Education 2006:35(3);285–300.

Miracles, monsters and disturbances

Elio Caccavale
Michael Reiss

Modern science challenges many well-established borders. Genetics in particular raises the prospect of merging species, transferring DNA between species or questioning the very essence of a species. It is creating new opportunities, limited, perhaps, only by our imagination – or what we believe is acceptable: some real or potential applications of new technologies often raise a deep sense of unease. Although rational science can describe what is possible, perhaps, suggest *Elio Caccavale* and *Michael Reiss*, only the arts and humanities can truly articulate what the future might look like, by unleashing a creative process that integrates an emotional as well as a literal perspective on imagined future worlds.

The idea that there is a simple and obvious distinction between different species is deeply rooted in our culture. Yet modern biotechnology, with its ability to create chimeras (mixing embryonic cells from different species) and genetic hybrids (incorporating genetic material from different species into a particular genome), makes the self-evidence of this distinction problematic. Scientists can now manipulate the genetic information that plays a part in the developmental process of all life forms. Using sophisticated recombinant-DNA and cell-fusion processes, genetic information from unrelated species can be inserted, deleted or even stitched and fused together, creating forms of life that have never before existed. This has provoked deep anxiety among many people, an anxiety that has been variously described as a rejection of the 'unnatural' or a fear of the 'alien' or the 'dangerous'. On the other hand, from ancient times, our culture has been fascinated by creatures that combine varied features from different animals, or animals mixed with humans, such as griffins and centaurs. Such hybrids, or monstrous creatures, challenge our usual sense of categorisation and provide us with the stimulus for thinking about the truly fundamental aspects of both biological and physical human nature.

Increasingly, the news media and popular culture are alerting the public to the heated dialogue that is underway about what our near future might become. Daily, the miraculous scientific predictions and breakthroughs that were once the subject of science fiction are announced as realities. Each new announcement triggers hopes and fears and guarantees further debate among humanitarians, profit seekers, legal experts, ethicists, politicians and the public. Science and art collaborations could have an important role in this ongoing exploration, creating images that literally give shape to intangible and complex concepts. Working with new languages and images, they raise questions about the social, cultural, ecological, economic and ethical implications of science breakthroughs. The works of many artists informed by science investigate issues and concerns triggered by the modification of nature, and provide the public with an opportunity to pay closer attention to advances in science and to reflect upon the boundaries between science and the human imagination. They consider how we shape nature to meet our desires and demands, manipulating genetic make-ups and changing the form and productivity of animals and other organisms.

This intersection of contemporary science and contemporary artistic responses to such science opens up new educational spaces. Issues to do with the crossing of species boundaries and other sorts of genetic transformation are rich in educational potential. In part this is because such issues, while current, tap into deeper fears about losing what it is that makes us human and distinguishes us from other animals. In large measure too it is simply that science here is seen as it operates at the frontier of knowledge, rather than in the rather ossified form it generally takes in school science lessons. This provides an open-endedness to science that can be attractive to many for whom science is all too often boring or irrelevant. This chapter therefore seems to explore how education about science can draw richly on practices in art and design. Such practices can help learners explore the moral and social implications of new technologies and enable all of us to reflect on what is possible and what is desirable.

Science here is seen as it operates at the frontier of knowledge, rather than in the rather ossified form it generally takes in school science lessons

Above:
Eduardo Kac with Alba.

Evitables and inevitables

Collaborations between artists and scientists in education can draw on related work in laboratories and in the cultural sector. In these contexts, science and art collaborations quite often speculate about these new parameters of life and these expressions of scientific creativity with a mixture of awe and concern. Two closely related categories of artist working on hybridity can be identified: the evitables and the inevitables. A good example of the inevitables is Chicago artist Eduardo Kac,[1] who is known worldwide for his 'GFP Bunny'. The project consists of a GM rabbit named Alba, which was created with the help of French scientists[2] who injected the DNA for green fluorescent protein (GFP) of a Pacific Northwest jellyfish into the fertilised egg of an albino rabbit. The project comprises not only the creation of the fluorescent rabbit but also the public dialogue generated by this and the integration of the transgenic animal into society. Kac had intended to take custody of Alba, but because of growing concerns for her welfare and the (allegedly) potentially devastating effect the bunny would have on the ecosystem if she were to escape and reproduce, she was not released to Kac.

The idea of taking Alba into a domestic environment places genetic engineering in a social context in which the relationship between the private and the public spheres are negotiated. In other words, biotechnology, the private realm of family life and the social domain of public opinion are discussed in relation to one another. Kac has created digital manipulated photos (photo) of the rabbit so that she appears greener than is physically possible even for the Pacific jellyfish itself. Reproductions of the photo of Kac's green rabbit have been published in newspapers and exhibited in art galleries, and have no doubt contributed to the public engagement discourse on transgenic animals.

The ecologist Ignacio Chapela[3] points out that the rabbit photographs were digitally altered and explained that rabbits cannot have green corneas. Chapela does not make this point to

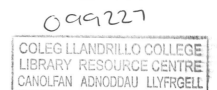

comment on Kac's project, but rather to argue that green fluorescing rabbit pets are not inevitable. By pointing this out Chapela shows that the press don't mind about the veracity of an image – a digital manipulation is better if it is more sensational – and that the French scientist's refusal to release Alba from the laboratory is an example of this very sociocultural phenomenon.

The Australian artist Patricia Piccinini[4] is an example of the evitables. She creates humanoid sculptural installations to confront us with images of a future where human gene technology gives us the ability to create genetic hybrids and chimeras. One particular project shown at the Australian Pavilion at the Venice Biennale in 2003 included a variety of bizarre, genetically engineered beings that are strikingly different from what we know but, at the same time, strangely familiar. 'The Young Family' sculpture series consisted of a human sow primate with arms and legs who suckles a litter of human piglets as she lounges on a leather sofa. The mother's tarnished skin has the unsightly wrinkles, red blotches, moles and imperfections we might find on our own bodies. Her hands and feet could belong to a grandfather. Human traits aside, she looks more or less like a pig – despite the strikingly tender maternal gaze she casts upon her offspring.

While 'The Young Family' may be warning the public, it also radically overestimates the control we have over biological systems. In her art Piccinini creates organisms that cannot feasibly be produced in actuality, producing a delusion of comprehensive genetic knowledge and control. It is what we do not know that is truly dangerous. Her sculptures have the opposite effect of their intended shock-and-awe tactic; by contrast, actual images of genetically engineered organisms look banal. Think, for instance, of ordinary-looking goats produced by the Canadian biotech company Nexia Biotechnologies.[5] Nexia has spliced spider genes responsible for webs (one of the strongest fibres known in nature) into the genome of a goat. When the goat's milk is processed, the

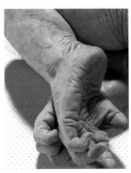

Above:
'The Young Family' by Australian artist Patricia Piccinini.

result is BioSteel, a substance that can be spun into a thread that has the tensile strength and flexibility of a super spider web. The potential applications range from medical applications to bullet-proofing and sports equipment.

Hybridity

In our own work on hybridity, biotechnology can be seen as an experimental ground where the most advanced technological innovation clashes with more human aspects and concerns, such as ethics and social conduct, and where the evitable meets the inevitable. The myBio project[6] exhibited at the Science Learning Centre London explores the emergence of biological hybrids in biotechnologies, and our human, personal, moral, aesthetic and sociocultural responses to them. The creation of any kind of hybrid begins to challenge species boundaries – in particular, an entirely new resonance on how we learn and form categories about 'the human' and 'the animal' is brought about. Our work on hybridity builds on recent creativity and scholarship in design, bioethics and historical and anthropological studies in the human, the animal and the monstrous, providing tools for investigating our moral, social, cultural and personal responses to the strange and different in human biology and also 'transhuman' creatures. The result is an increase in teasing out and provoking discussion regarding genetically modified human–animal hybrids in existing and near future biotechnology. In particular, what is sought is an understanding of the relationship between children's learning in the categories of animal/human and the extent to which such categories can be considered merely contingent and revisable in the light of technological change.

There are two main areas of research interests that have contributed to the outcomes of our collaboration. The first investigated the emergence of biological hybrids in biotechnologies, with particular respect to the breeding of GM animals and xenotransplantation. Focusing on the implications of the techniques that have already entered the public domain, we examined the impact of such innovations as the BioSteel goat developed by Nexia Technologies, the transgenic ornamental fish developed by Taikong Corp.,[7] the low-fat pork in pigs developed by Kinki University[8] in Japan, the transgenic pigs for xenotransplantation developed by NexTran,[9] the featherless chickens developed by the Hebrew University School of Agriculture[10] in Israel (right) and the Enviropig[11] developed by the University of Guelph in Canada.

Above:
Featherless chickens developed by the Hebrew University School of Agriculture.

The second area of research interest focused on the educational material culture that uses the playful and abstract language of educational dolls to help facilitate children's understanding of biologically, socially and culturally complex concepts. A wide range of such dolls have been developed: sex educational dolls, race equality educational dolls, disabled educational dolls, medical condition educational dolls. As yet, though, there is a remarkable dearth of information as to the consequences of using such material. A search on Google Scholar for "educational dolls" (22 September 2007) revealed just 12 hits – all of which are for patents. Our supposition, despite the current lack of scholarly evidence for this, is that dolls may be powerful enablers of exploration and learning. We note that the value of puppets in science education is beginning to be explored.[12]

Learning from companies and organisations that produce educational dolls and using their established visual imagery, we made 12 myBio dolls that could symbolise possible biofutures and introduce children to the emergence of biological hybrids. The dolls include: myBio boy and myBio pig, which demonstrate the physical transfer of the organ from the animal to the human; myBio bunny, myBio glowing fish and myBio jellyfish glow bright green when illuminated with a UV light, demonstrating how scientists have used GFP as a fluorescent indicator for monitoring gene expression in living organisms; myBio reactor cow shows how cows can produce proteins in their milk for pharmaceutical drugs

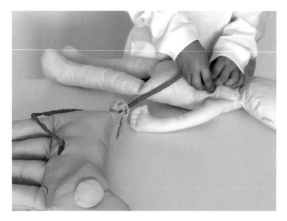

Above:
Oncology Buddy –
Shadow Buddies Foundation.

Left from top:
MyBio xenotransplant,
myBio reactor and
myBio spider goat.

(this is symbolised by the 'milk thread' attached to the cow's udders); and myBio goat has a spider web attached to the udders, demonstrating one animal making the natural product of another. We have used the myBio dolls to present scientific information through the channel of the narrative. Starting with a series of 'What if?' stories, the narrative process gives children a common language for talking about biotechnology. "Suppose that your life could be saved by a pig, what would happen to you and the pig?" or "Imagine you could have a glow-in-the-dark rabbit, would you relate to such a rabbit differently than a conventional one?"

We are particularly interested in children's responses to the impact of biotechnologies, affected as they are by the aesthetic of new scientific creations (think for instance of a glow-in-the-dark bunny) that can make the concept of hybridity exciting. Much of the academic reaction to recent biotechnological developments across species boundaries has been ethical. Careful ethical reflection and analysis is important, but we believe that artistic presentations and reactions have much to offer. In particular, they can be more open-ended, demanding much of the viewer, and then they rely on faculties other than the cerebral, thus engaging us on a greater number of levels and facilitating the tangibility of abstract concepts. Here, then, we see art not as a decoration of science but as a necessary partner if we are better to imagine how we were, how we are and how we will or want to be.

As part of the myBio project we also instituted a workshop with medical and product design students at Central Saint Martins College of Art and Design (part of the University of the Arts London). The students worked together in interdisciplinary groups. Their objective was to explore animals by proposing hypothetical hybrids and animal products. The hybrids proposed had to perform in new ways, and, as such, create new effects, phenomena and behaviours. After creating their hybrids, the groups were asked to develop hypothetical, yet feasible, social scenarios based on their

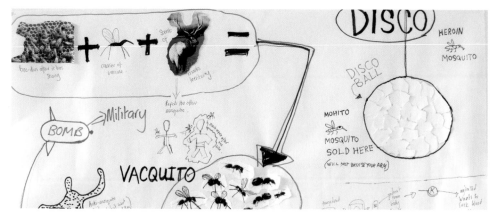

Above:
Work produced by the student hybrids workshop at Central Saint Martins College of Art and Design.

initial ideas, that is to consider what people would do with their hybrids. How would new social behaviours emerge around their hybrids? What would be the physical consequences of their hybrids? And what new points of interface would exist between the hybrids and people?

Although none of the participants knew each other prior to the event, there was free and fertile exchange of ideas and roles throughout the workshop. This led to a breaking down of traditional interdisciplinary boundaries, thereby facilitating an open and inspirational dialogue between design, art and science. The students responded positively to the workshop experience and they have expressed strong interest in being involved in other sciart workshops. We see every reason to expect that similar responses would be found in schools and colleges with students across the 11–19 age range, because it would enable them to draw on their own ideas and subsequently to reflect on these and debate them.

Miracles or monsters?

The word 'miracle' comes from the Latin *miraculum*, meaning an object of wonder. To this day the word retains its two main uses: on the one hand, a technical, theological term meaning an event that cannot be explained by the laws of nature and therefore provides evidence for some divine (i.e. supernatural) intervention; on the other, its more everyday usage simply meaning something 'remarkable' or 'wonderful'. This everyday term is nearly always understood positively, so that we say it was a miracle that a family survived a horrendous car crash, not that it was a miracle that another family sheltering under a tree in a thunderstorm was killed by lightning.

It is the everyday usage that is more important, of course, in the new technologies – we are not talking here about the formal proof of three important miracles that the Roman Catholic Church requires before the process of canonisation can be completed. However, the everyday and the eternal cannot so easily be separated; we stand in awe of non-supernatural miracles even when they are rooted in the realities of nature. Such miracles challenge our understanding and enlarge our vision.

But in many people's eyes – and one of the advantages of sciart dialogue is its shift from the cerebral and verbal to the visual and splanchnic – tomorrow's biotechnological products threaten to be monsters not miracles. Monsters, like miracles, come in various forms. But just as we see miracles as generally positive, for all the neutrality of the etymology of the term, so monsters are generally perceived to be negative. Like miracles, monsters are rare, but when perceived they shock, they terrify, they disgust.

Historically, as Harriet Ritvo argues in her suitably titled *The Platypus and the Mermaid: And other figments of the classifying imagination*,[13] only a small divergence from what seemed natural sufficed to make a monster – and the same is true today. It can be a thin line between ugliness and monstrosity. However, ugliness sits within the normal range; a monster sits apart. A naked cat may be ugly in many people's eyes but a lamb with five legs is a monster, a 'sport of nature'. It is this 'apartness' that is crucial in understanding the common, visceral reaction to that which is monstrous – a term applied not only to entities but also to actions. So slavery, child warfare and the force-feeding of geese to produce *pâté de foie gras* can (should) be described as monstrous as they sit outside our common perceptions of what it should be to be a human, a child or a goose.

As is well known, monsters fascinate. We know of the awful times Joseph Merrick, the Elephant Man, lived though because of his

Above:
Work and participants at the
Central Saint Martins hybrids
workshop.

deformity but while we may regard with condescension the thought of Victorian freak shows, we do well to remember the contemporary fascination with conjoined twins – e.g. Abby and Britty Hensel, Lori and George (aka Dori and Reba) Schappell – as evidenced by the many TV documentaries and newspaper and magazine articles they inspire. Such examples can be both attractive and repellent to young people; certainly, they question our existing classifications.

Broadening from unusual humans to unusual animals, monsters that failed to sit tidily within established categories caused problems for those taxonomists keen to produce an ordered classification. As is well known, the arrival of the first specimens of the duck-billed platypus (*Ornithorhynchus anatinus*) in the UK at the end of the 18th century so astonished naturalists that the specimens were widely regarded as fakes. It was presumed that someone had sewn a duck's beak onto the body of a beaver-like animal. Today we understand the platypus as one of the five extant species of monotremes (the other four are echidnas) found in Australia. Uniquely among mammals, monotremes lay eggs rather than producing live young; they also, and again incongruously, have electroreceptors to help them detect their prey. Adult platypuses are also most unusual among mammals in being venomous.

Disturbances

The more bullish of today's biologists are fond of saying that we are on the threshold of a new age; that contemporary applications of biology are about to make the same sort of difference to our ways of living that the agricultural revolutions of several millennia ago, the industrial revolution of the 19th century and the communications revolution of the late 20th century made. Analyses of such prophecies have tended to focus on whether or not such a biorevolution would be desirable. Would it lead to improved human health and increased crop yields or to new diseases and the extinction of certain plant species? Would it result in more or less human happiness, to greater or less inequality among people? But there is another way of examining the implications of developments in today's biology, and that is to look at their meanings. What might be the effects of the widespread use of genetic engineering, cloning, stem cell technology and so on on how we understand ourselves and the rest of nature? Such questions about the significance of new technologies received a powerful articulation before the advent of genetic engineering from Heidegger, who argued that in technology we make objects according to some blueprint that we determine. We design things to satisfy our purposes rather than allow our purposes to be affected by, and find creative expression through, the qualities of the objects themselves.[14]

For this reason an approach that explores the emergence of biological hybrids in biotechnologies, and our human, personal, moral, aesthetic and sociocultural responses to them, is to be welcomed. Nowhere are these issues raised more sharply than in the new 'hybrids' of genetically modified animals. It is important to remember that not all genetic engineering entails moving genes between species. For example, the genetic engineering of yeasts to 'improve' breads and beers involves using the tools of genetic engineering to move genes between strains or varieties of yeast but still within the one species. Here genetic engineering is being used to speed up a process that could equally be carried out by conventional breeding – the essence of a biological species being that within it individuals are able to breed among themselves. Unsurprisingly, this use of genetic engineering has raised little controversy and – more importantly for the questions considered here – little disquiet.

Those instances of genetic engineering of most concern both to the general public and to members of pressure groups opposed to genetic engineering involve the movement of genes between

Above:
The Central Saint Martins
hybrids workshop participants.

species, often between completely unrelated species. For example, genes from scorpions have been moved into viruses in an attempt to make such viruses more toxic to insect pests, and genes from humans have been moved into pigs in the hope that organs from these pigs might be suitable for (xeno)transplantation.

In any useful sense, moving genes from scorpions to viruses, and from humans to pigs, is unnatural. The question is, how concerned should we be at this breaching of species boundaries? Does it matter that plant crops contain bacterial or animal genes if the result is that their yields are greater? Does it matter that certain bacteria confined to fermenters in pharmaceutical factories contain human genes if the result is that life-saving and health-restoring medicines, such as insulin, are produced? Does it matter that pigs are being genetically engineered with human genes in the hope that their internal organs may be used for human transplants? And, almost irrespective of whether it matters, in some absolute sense or not (if such a perspective exists), how do we feel about the dissolutions of these boundaries?

One interesting psychological point is that as we grow up the boundaries between species help us to organise our understanding of the natural world. Children learn from their infancy about living things in their immediate environment. In particular, they learn about animals, learning both to recognise different types of animals and what their basic names are. It has been argued that the concepts 'animal' and 'plant' are fundamental ontological categories – that is, categories used by children to organise their perceptions of the world in which they live. Certainly for most children, animals form a significant part of the world around them, whether as wildlife, pets or zoomorphic toys. It is therefore unsurprising that names for familiar animals form a large part of the vocabulary of young children.

Boundaries serve to divide entities into categories; in this way a boundary enables classification. It can make us secure and helps us structure our world. Of course, such security may be prejudiced. The strict boundaries that once divided men and women in terms of how each of us might spend our time are changing fast. Activities such as cross-dressing make little sense to some people, are deeply disturbing to others, are political statements by some and are essential to a few. One can ask whether it is wrong to eat animals that have been genetically engineered to contain human genes.[15] This question may soon become pressing as the number of animals with human genes continues to increase.

At one pole are those who argue that eating an animal, or a plant, into which a human gene has been inserted has nothing whatever to do with cannibalism. Cannibalism is about eating human flesh, not eating minute amounts of DNA that once came from just one of the 30 000 or so human genes and is now merely a copy of that original human gene. Further, every baby who breastfeeds eats large amounts of another human's (i.e. its mother's) DNA.

Those who object to inserting human genes into animals that are subsequently used for human consumption may argue that the parallels with cannibalism cannot so lightly be dismissed. Although Imutran, one of the companies at one point actively engaged in xenotransplantation research, has argued, "This involves changing only 0.001 per cent of the genetic make-up of the pig,"[16] it could be argued that the actual percentage of change is not of prime importance. After all, if one is unfaithful to one's spouse on only 0.5 per cent of nights, is this ten times better than if one is unfaithful on 5 per cent of nights? Reverting to traditional

Those who object to inserting human genes into animals that are subsequently used for human consumption may argue that the parallels with cannibalism cannot so lightly be dismissed.

anthropological concepts, one either exists in a state of purity or impurity – there are no halfway positions, no no-man's-lands gradually to be traversed. Similarly, just because a baby less than a year or so old does certain things with its mother doesn't make it right for the rest of us to do those same things with its mother.

We need new ways of exploring the meanings raised by genetic engineering and other modern biotechnologies. Rational words are needed but are not enough. This is why an approach through art and design can be so valuable. The two of us are particularly interested in the potential of such artefacts to help both students and teachers develop their thinking and, as importantly, their affective responses. Most of us now need fewer boundaries than our ancestors did. Just as symbols (e.g. blood) can be, in different contexts, either defiling or sanctifying, so a boundary can serve either to maintain order and strengthen that which it encloses or to lead to disunity. Increasingly people find themselves uncomfortable with boundaries that seem to lack a rational basis. Why shouldn't people of the same sex be able to get married if they want to? Why shouldn't women be front-line soldiers? And yet, are all boundaries to be crossed, all divisions eroded if they cannot be defended on rational grounds? Is incest between freely consenting adults to be permitted if they use reliable contraceptives? Is it morally right to move genes between species? And whether it is or is not, how do we feel about it? As Catherine Booth said, "If we are to better the future we must disturb the present."

1 www.ekac.org.
2 Louis-Marie Houdebine, Reproduction and Developmental Biology Unit, National Institute of Agronomic Research, France.
3 www.cnr.berkeley.edu/chapelalab/.
4 www.patriciapiccinini.net.
5 www.nexiabiotech.com/en/01_tech/01-bst.php.
6 www.eliocaccavale.com/mybio.html.
7 www.azoo.com.tw.
8 http://ccpc01.cc.kindai.ac.jp/english/index.htm.
9 www.nex-tran.com.
10 http://ksvm.agri.huji.ac.il.
11 www.uoguelph.ca/enviropig/.
12 www.informaworld.com/smpp/content~content=a780865755~db=all.
13 Ritvo (1997).
14 Heidegger (1977).
15 Reiss (2003).
16 Novartis Imutran (1999).

Bibliography

Heidegger M. The Question Concerning Technology and Other Essays. Transl. William Lovitt. New York: Harper Colophon; 1977.

Novartis Imutran. Animal Welfare: Xenotransplantation – helping to solve the global organ shortage. Cambridge: Imutran Ltd; 1999.

Reiss MJ. Is it right to move genes between species? A theological perspective. In C Deane-Drummond et al. (eds). Re-ordering Nature: Theology, society and the new genetics. London: T&T Clark; 2003. pp. 138–50.

Ritvo H. The Platypus and the Mermaid: And other figments of the classifying imagination. Cambridge, MA: Harvard University Press; 1997.

The myBio project is realised through the collaboration of Elio Caccavale (Royal College of Art) with Professor Richard Ashcroft (Queen Mary, University of London) and Professor Michael Reiss (Institute of Education, University of London).

Using illusions to teach children about the science and art of seeing

Sara J Downham
R Beau Lotto
David Strudwick

The principal way that people draw information from the world is through the visual system. Yet the seemingly coherent view we gain about the world is a creation of our brain, and not necessarily an accurate representation of how things really are. This can be vividly illustrated by illusions, which have delighted and bemused for generations. But as *Sara J Downham, R Beau Lotto* and *David Strudwick* point out, illusions offer the potential not just to teach about visual perception but also to act as an illustration of the brain's role as an active interpreter rather than a passive observer.

An illusion is the phenomenon of perceiving something different from what is physically there. This chapter will describe why illusions may be a useful tool in the classroom for learning how and why we see what we do, and consider how the exploration of illusion encourages children's (and adults') curiosity, creativity and confidence (the three 'C's). The chapter is divided into three sections. The first describes the science of seeing illusions: why we see them and what it tells us about how the brain works. The second section describes one example of applying this scientific understanding in the context of an art project in a primary school classroom. The third section explains the importance of using illusions to break with some received methods of learning and teaching by emphasising the ambiguity of learned and inherited truths and conventions, with the implicit aim of encouraging children to respond more empathetically to the world around them.

The science of seeing

The 19th-century French painter Delacroix exclaimed: "Give me the mud of the streets and I will turn it into the luscious flesh of a woman, if you will allow me to surround it as I please." Goethe in the mid-19th century 'discovered' that a grey shadow appears anything but grey when surrounded by light of a different colour. The effects of the surround on our perceptions of colour are well known and have been much explored by philosophers and artists for centuries. What remained unknown until recently is why we see illusions at all, or more generally, why context matters. Answering this question is the topic here, and explaining why the answer is important for models of pedagogy and learning is the point of the chapter. When you open your eyes you are aware of objects, shapes, shadows, locations in space, a relatively stable world (even though your head may be moving); you see people, dogs, trees, the blue sky and the yellow sun...a coherent whole and you do so immediately... or at least it feels that way. But is this what your eyes see? Not at all – and this is important! What your eyes see are objectless, complex patterns of light. More accurately, your eyes see *completely ambiguous*, objectless, complex patterns of light, patterns of light that could – literally – mean anything. This is because images of the world are not the world itself.

There are many differences between images that fall onto the eye and the world that creates those images. For instance, the retinal image does not represent the colours of surfaces and illuminants directly, but only indirectly. The reason is that surfaces cannot be seen unless they are illuminated: no light and the world disappears; turn on the lights, and the light passes through the air, bouncing off surfaces in its path until it eventually hits the back of the eye. When the light hits a surface, its spectral composition changes according to how well the surface reflects the light's different constituent wavelengths. This means that the light that the eyes see is determined by the 'colour' of a surface and the 'colour' of its illumination. Change the colour of an object's illuminant – by placing it in the darkness of a shadow, the yellow of sunlight or the blue of skylight, for example – and the quality of light hitting the eye from that object will change even though the object is physically unchanged itself. Since a blue object under yellow light will look the same to the eyes as a yellow object under blue light, and similarly a dark grey surface under bright light will reflect the same amount of light to the eye as a light grey surface under dim light, each image the eyes see could – literally – mean any of an infinite combination of objects and illuminants. Clearly, then, if you are to see effectively, seeing the retinal image is not going to do it: there simply isn't enough information in the retinal image. So how, then, do we see? How does the brain translate the ambiguous images of the world that fall onto the eye into perceptions that will be used to influence our behaviour? The brain can use only information that it has direct access to: the surrounding context and what that contextual information meant for behaviour in the past. Put another way, the brain solves the ambiguity of images because it has evolved the ability to find useful patterns in images, and to associate those patterns with previous behaviour that accord with past experience.

Our interpretation of language is an example of the power of this fundamentally empirical process of seeing. Like images on the retina, letter strings are, of themselves, meaningless. The letter string:

'H W AR Y U RE ADI G THI?'

means nothing. And yet most of you will read something coherent in it. Why? Because your brain, through its past interaction with the world (in this case the world of language), retains in its architecture an understanding of English. So while there is no a priori reason to put any letter between the 'H' and the 'W' in the above letter string, because it was useful to put an O there in the past, you reflexively do so again here, which is why you read the word 'HOW'. The same is true when you see colour.

Look at the small 'spots' in figure 1, which reflect the same amount of light to the eye. The two – not surprisingly – also look the same. But consider the fact that these two dots could actually have arisen from many different possible real-world sources. For instance, rather than arising from similar surfaces under similar lights, they could just as well have arisen from a dark surface in bright light on the one hand, or a light surface in dim light on the other. What happens if we provide contextual information that is consistent with these possibilities?

Well...look at the cube in figure 2. There are 25 tiles on its top surface that appear to be under direct light, and 25 tiles on the side of the cube that appear to be in shadow. There is a central tile on each of these two surfaces. On the illuminated surface this central tile appears brown, but bright orange on the shadowed surface. And yet these two are in fact the same tiles from figure 1. That is to say, the actual 'reality' of the scene is that the two tiles reflect the same amount to the eye, as shown in the 'mask', but this is not what you see. Instead you see what would have been useful to see in the past: that the tiles are different.

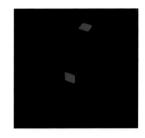

From top:
Figure 1: The 'spots' reflect the same amount of light to the eye and look the same.

Figure 2: The central tile on the illuminated surface appears darker brown than the central tile on the shaded surface, yet they are the same tiles shown in figure 1.

Beau Lotto

The art of seeing

Illusions tell us how the brain works. It constructs what it knows by searching for useful patterns in sensory information and then associating those patterns with a past record of their behavioural relevance. Which means that the brain is innately a creative and curious machine that evolved to continually redefine normality, a 'normality' that is necessarily contextual and historical, and on which one's perceptual truths are based. This point is relevant to all aspects of human thought, and can (and should) be explored at an intuitive level in the classroom through art.

There are a number of ways of engaging children with this point. One way is by enabling children to build physical models of illusions that are typically only seen in books or on the web. With these models in hand one can then explore why it is we see what we do. Another approach is to give children the opportunity to actively engage with the creative processes by which we actually construct our perceptual and conceptual truths, which – as described above – underlies why 'context is everything'. Here we describe an example of the latter approach, which took place in 2007 at Blackawton Primary School in Devon with five-to-six-year-old children. The school's head is David Strudwick – co-author of this chapter, and the workshop was undertaken as a collaboration between Beau Lotto and visual artist Sara Downham (also authors of this chapter).

The first day focused on 'the patterns we see', beginning in the children's immediate environment: the classroom. Before starting, the children were gathered together on the carpet, where the afternoon's activities were explained. There we elicited from them their understanding of what we might mean by 'the patterns we see'. Their ideas and descriptions were written on the board, and were discussed as a group. A typical relationship was between pattern and surface texture. An abstract notion was that a pattern was something that repeated across space (though that the repetition need not be exact, or even made up of all the same material).

The children were then put into several small groups and in those groups the game was to find as many visual patterns as possible, and re-create them using paint, pen and paper. Note that the aim wasn't to draw the objects in the classroom, but to represent the patterns that make up objects and to capture the spaces in between. Next the children were taken outside, where they repeated the task: observing and discovering patterns in nature, again drawing them on paper and – where possible – bringing the objects they had chosen back to class. When back in the classroom, they reassembled in their groups and, using words and pictures, they explained to the rest of the class the patterns they had found. Particularly imaginative examples included the branching patterns of trees, the texture of grass, the repetition of the carpet tiles, yellow lines on the road, the symmetry of a face, the stripes of a bumblebee, and the repetition of window, frame, window, frame of the school bus (as well as the tread on its tyres). It was a highly enjoyable activity – led largely by the children – that fostered their ability to observe, and resulted in abstract drawings and paintings. This emphasis on observing and re-creating patterns gave the children a fuller sense of the world around them.

The second day followed a similar programme to the first, with the exception that the focus was on the patterns we hear. As before, the children were initially gathered together on the carpet, and after explaining to them what was going to happen during the next couple of hours, we asked them to describe what we might mean by 'the patterns we hear'. Repetition of sound was the principle description. We then elicited from them examples of natural and artificial sound patterns, which we listed on the board: the lapping of waves, the dripping of a leaky tap, the running of a horse, the call of a bird, the beating of a wind turbine. After making this list, the children were encouraged to use their hands and feet, and were given instruments, sticks, books and so on to use to re-create some of these patterns. They were also given the chance to use these instruments (as well as the floor, whistling, humming, clapping, etc.) to create their own natural-esque patterns (both individually and in groups). This led on to discussions of music, or more generally to talking about 'the created pattern': the beating of the drum, the strum of a guitar, rhythm and beat, and thereby relating musical concepts to acoustic patterns that occur naturally. We also provided the children with examples of different kinds of musical pattern, and – as before – the children were given the chance to make their own music.

On the third day the children gathered on the carpet – this time in a circle, where we revisited the ideas and experiences of the previous two days. We then began a process of eliciting from them the potential relationship between the patterns we see and patterns we hear: What might the stripes on Misha's shirt sound like? What about the branching pattern of the tree outside the window? Or black-and-white stripes of a zebra? The children volunteered many ideas for relationships: "I think the petal pattern of flowers would sound like this…", "I think the pattern of carpet might sound like this…". Tempo was strongly related to the frequency of the pattern, though they also incorporated colours (or more generally the colour contrast) into their translations, with strong colours usually

sounding louder than weaker – less saturated – colours. The sound of alternating thin black-and-white lines on a zebra, for example, had a higher tempo and sounded louder than the thick black-and-white shadows across the wall.

The children were then organised into smaller groups, and given a large black piece of paper, upon which they were asked to create their own visual pattern using paint, paper cut-outs, pen and pencil (called 'mark-making'). Their task was to think less about the visual pattern in terms of what it 'looked like', and more in terms of what it might sound like. In essence, the children were being asked to create a piece of music, not with notes on a stave, but with colour (which we call a 'colour score'). One could literally hear the children 'humming their image' as they created it, all of which are shown in figure 3.

Each child's colour score was then photographed with a digital camera, and sent to the lottolab in London, where they were uploaded into 'Synesthetic', which translates colours into musical notes in space and time. To get a sense of this program, imagine a horizontal line a few pixels high scanning down an image from top to bottom. Now imagine that this line is made up of 32 consecutive boxes, and that each box represents a musical instrument – a violin, a piano, drum, etc. The note each instrument plays at any point in time is directly related to the average colour in its box at that location of the image. As the line scans down the image, the colour of each box changes, and how it changes depends, of course, on the child's image. This process changes the instruments' note in time, which means that time is encoded along the image's vertical axis and tone across the image's horizontal axis. This means that each image is literally the score of a musical composition. The instruments (or ensemble) included violins, cellos, woodwind and brass instruments. The Synesthetic program then takes each digitised image, scans it from top to bottom, translates each pixel into a note, plays that note in stereo, with the sound arising in

Left:
Figure 3: A 'colour score' created by children asked to create a piece of music with colour.
Beau Lotto

space according to its horizontal location across the page, and then saves the whole process as a QuickTime movie on a DVD. These movies were then given to each child.

The results were fabulous. Not just in the sounds and music created, but also in the children's responses to their own and to their classmates' compositions. Not only did each child want everyone else to hear their composition, but also they wanted to hear the compositions of others. In other words the children took pride in what they had created, as well as in the works of their classmates, partly because the activity was so novel that they had no basis for competition.

But did the children learn what we had hoped they would? The answer seems to be yes. For weeks afterwards, the children who took part continued to discuss with each other and the teacher the sounds that different visual patterns might make (and vice versa). Parents, too, positively reported to the headteacher that their child, "who was not previously artistic", was coming home and "doing art". In other words the children continued to apply the idea of actively exploring their environment and in doing so finding and creating new (abstract) patterns of relationships therein. Thus, the objective of getting the children to look beyond the obvious – to consider the relationships between things, by providing them with a wholly new kind of experience, one that was both very interesting and resulted in a high-status outcome – fostered the brain's innate process of redefining normality.

Illusion as metaphor in eduction
Illusions show us that the mind is an evolved machine that continually redefines normality. It is a machine that innately searches for, and creates, relationships and patterns from sensory information, and this information is then used to guide behaviour. Thus, illusions ultimately tell us who we are as individuals: creators, defined by our history of interaction. For the world of education

and learning, the important suggestion is that it is not the event that defines us, but that we are defined by our interpretations of our experiences.

Fleas in a jar learn that they can only jump so high without banging their heads. As a result, when the jar is removed, their jumping behaviour is constrained to the height of the jar. Children who are teased in lessons for being wrong experience the equivalent of banging their head on the roof of a jar. The process contributes to their overall history of experience, which necessarily contributes to their future understanding of the world and of themselves. Most commonly such children – understandably – conclude that they are no good at particular lessons with the result that the next jump is 'safer'...one less high, or at least a level lower than their potential! Such an association can become self-reinforcing, since – especially in social and emotional areas of learning – we tend to see only those patterns that support our world-view. In other words, if you believe that you are no good at something, you will come to see the world through that filter, finding, collecting and creating information that supports this 'truth'. This process of creation and re-affirmation can lead to irrational, but very real, fears that stop us from attempting new experiences, of seeing things differently. Instead one adopts strategies for dealing with these fears. For example, children are often amazed when they learn that others in the class use all kinds of strategies to avoid the challenge of a difficult task: when we are really learning it is often uncomfortable, since our view of the world is being challenged!

The importance of illusions in breaking negative pattern-matching has tremendous potential. The process of seeing illusion as metaphor has the capacity to foster a different kind of learning: 'this is how you see it now, but with a bit of courage it is possible to see it differently'. By supporting children through physical instances where the same object can be perceived differently, children can be led away from the admittedly more comfortable black-and-white view of the world to the more challenging but also more enlightening realisation of the greys in between. The learner can be shown in real terms that their perceived truths are not necessarily *the* reality, but *one* reality among others. In this way, illusions can help learners to become positively excited about getting things wrong, since it is through 'getting things wrong' that we begin to see things differently, or at least more wholly. By going beyond the 'refrigerated facts' of the black-and-white, towards the more open-ended view of relationships, children can develop the ability to respond empathically to others by considering the potential meanings of an event, action or object that is outside of their own histories.

www.lottolab.org

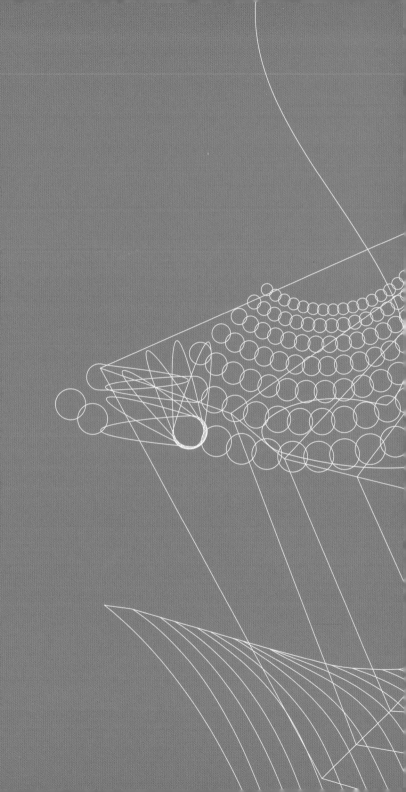

Introducing space

Simon Parry

The spaces of education can, for many people, be very vividly drawn. They are delineated by the symbols of the classroom, the school or the university: rows of chairs, blackboards or whiteboards, libraries, corridors. Modern influences may be seen in computer rooms, an interactive whiteboard or equipment for practical science experiments. But, in many respects, the spaces would be recognisable to the parents, grandparents and great-grandparents of today's children. However, experiences of space are changing.

The various manifestations of globalisation have given rise to global culture, global markets and global information networks. The operations of global capitalism and multinational companies are overlaid onto national systems of political representation and state control of public services and regulation of national industry. Political power at the level of the nation-state is juxtaposed with supranational political bodies such as the UN and the EU. Theorists refer to "cosmopolitan space" or "the space of flows" created by international relations and electronic or corporate networks (Archibugi and Held, 1995; Castells, 2000). In everyday life, global space is manifested through the constant movement of things and people. Shops stock fresh fruit that has travelled halfway round the world. Business can be conducted by phone or email with companies whose geographical location is dispersed or unclear to the customer. Those with the money and the right passports benefit from considerable international mobility for work or for leisure.

In the first chapter of this section, Stephen Heppell engages head-on with changing experiences of space, their impact on learning and their implications for the spaces of education. He outlines the challenge to policy makers and practitioners in education to keep up with the way he argues that "learning is changing" in the world. He refers to both the physical and metaphorical space of the corridor to embody a form of education that is outmoded in the 21st century, and criticises the linearity and constraining nature of thinking in corridors as well as the practical barriers to education presented by the systems and architecture of many school buildings. He calls for radical thinking in terms of the scale and size of learning institutions. For Heppell, it seems that solutions will be found from bridging disciplines and geographical space, from personalisation rather than uniformity in educational space and from the bottom up. His challenge is wide-ranging and provocative.

Most school and university students have a very strong sense of where they think science happens. It is a practice strongly associated with spaces of education and even with particular spaces in the institutions. Indeed, you can find school science labs all over the world that would bear a remarkable similarity to each other. While many scientists and non-scientists were inspired by their experiences during the time they spent in such places, most leave them behind on leaving school. Indeed many of those who use science in their everyday work have little use for Bunsen burners and test-tubes – the symbols of school scientific space – relying rather more on computing power as their principal tool. Other scientific professionals such as doctors, nurses and other health workers have to work in a variety of spaces and places, drawing on knowledge generated in laboratories but applying it in surgeries, clinics, hospitals, people's homes or workplaces. Scientific knowledge clearly travels between social settings and across geographical borders but it is not unaffected by the journey. The scientific facts may be the same in a high-tech Californian lab as in rural Africa, but people's relationship to them, the way they are applied and their impact on everyday life is likely to very different.

In the chapter by Simon Turley, Jeff Teare and Anthony Pinching, the idea of space is used both in a physical sense to refer to the spaces of the theatre, the rehearsal room, the clinic and the classroom, and also in the sense of disciplinary or expert space. They talk about their collective process of discovering each other's ways of working in terms of a journey through different "conceptual and technical expert spaces". Taking turns with the roles of "mountain-guide" and follower, they have explored the way different spaces situate science and human experience. Turley remarks on his surprise at being moved by a clinical narrative in a medical school lecture. Pinching notes the role of narrative and metaphor in the practice of clinicians. Motivated by the difficulties of patients suffering from a condition, CFS/ME, that is profoundly experienced but with a lack of a firm, disciplinary space of reference, they make use of the relative freedom provided by theatrical space to explore it in all its lived experience and scientific uncertainty. In *Something Somatic*, the demands on the playwright, Turley, were to stage the insubstantial: to present the complex workings of the body in dramatic space. In their earlier collaboration on *Seeing Without Light*, Turley and Pinching had started off with a dialogue around scientific accuracy but moved onto issues of situating the science in social contexts in the UK and Africa. The educational challenge in their use of dramatic space is encapsulated in Pinching's reference to the way performance can combine "distance for perspective" and "a new proximity of experience". Their reflections on their own interdisciplinary learning have profound implications for their and others' practice as educators in the theatre, the school and in the training of clinicians.

In the final chapter of the section, Anna Ledgard reflects on a highly experimental example of educational theatre-making in which there was a departure not only from conventional spaces of science education but also from expected artistic spaces. In the projects she discusses, there was an attempt by quirky and often surreal symbolic means to transform spaces for art and learning. Both *Visiting Time* and *Boychild* were created in places loaded with significance and symbolism of their own. In both cases the performances brought ideas and ways of seeing the world into the spaces, which had an indelible impact on the perception of these spaces by both performers and audiences. Through the pedagogical processes used by Mark Storor and the author in the creation of the performances, they tried to create safe, trusting spaces for raising big ideas and asking questions students might not normally be expected to ask in formal education settings. However, through the strong links between the collaborators and scientists and between the performance themes and scientific ideas, these projects demonstrated the possibility of linking formal and informal learning spaces in new ways and creating productive interactions between classroom-based learning and more experiential approaches.

All the practices discussed in this section, and indeed throughout the book, indicate potential for finding new places in which to engage with science outside the laboratory and the classroom. There is also a sense in these accounts that the incursion of scientific ideas into artistic space can make for a richer and more powerful cultural landscape. The journeys artists and scientists have made into each other's spaces and the journeys on which they have guided their students as educators suggest ways of making connections between different forms of knowledge. Such flexibility in the navigation of space may well prove essential in the globalised, interconnected world of the 21st century.

Bibliography
Archibugi D, Held D (eds). Cosmopolitan Democracy: An agenda for a new world order. Oxford: Polity; 1995.
Castells M. The Rise of the Network Society. Oxford: Blackwell; 2000.

Places to learn in the 21st century

Stephen Heppell

What should the learning spaces of the future look like? Those of the past, argues *Stephen Heppell*, have done little to encourage highly engaged learning. A radical reimagination of learning spaces is needed to reflect the reality of a globalised and networked world where teamwork is valued alongside individual endeavour, collaborators can be on a different continent, and people develop their own solutions. If education is too stuck in its ways to take a lead, empowered young people will reform things for themselves, exploiting the new technological tools that have already revolutionised their social world.

A school in Christchurch, New Zealand, is built with a lifespan of less than a decade; its students are all in place on day one and at that point the school roll is complete. In a school in Dudley, England, children study just one subject for a whole month, two years early, and complete their examination requirements before moving on to another subject the next month. In Bangkok, a community learning space atop a shopping mall is thronged with families, from young children to their grandparents. A tiny Caribbean school with a handful of children finds itself linked to a global network of other tiny schools as its scale becomes its greatest asset. In Minnesota, a school abandons timetables, subject headings and age phases, and finds that engagement leaps forward. An online global virtual school for those excluded from school finds re-engagement figures around 98 per cent, up from zero. A Tasmanian school, allegedly torched by its students, is rebuilt in a radical new way by a community, which sees learning rise phoenix-like from the ashes. In Australia, a school is built with barely any staffroom at all – "everyone here is a learner," they say. In the Cayman Islands, a large underperforming school is rapidly subdivided into four entirely new schools; names that children choose for these new schools include 'Leading Edge' and 'New Horizons'. In Iceland, a new school, with a roof waved like the Atlantic, offers small 'family' learning units.

This page and opposite: School science area designs produced for the Government's Project Faraday.

Clockwise from above: Demonstration area for East Barnet School, Hertfordshire. *DEGW*

Incident centre for Rednock School, Gloucestershire. *cube_design*

Bio-dome for Cramlington High School, Northumberland. *Waring & Netts Partnership*

Courtyard learning space for Bideford College, Devon. *White Design Associates*

In every case these radical departures from the staid old model of 20th-century education are also characterised by the extraordinary results they produce. Welcome to the world of 21st-century global learning.

Around the world, education is changing. Or perhaps more accurately, learning is changing, despite education. That in itself is news; traditionally, education has been characterised by a slowness to change, an inherent conservatism and a reluctance to climb on board the bandwagons of fashion or political fads, perhaps historically with good reason. Those fads have come and gone – who remembers the Initial Teaching Alphabet? – but since children

Big was beautiful, and the
realities of mass production
arguably clouded judgement
on more social matters so
that we overlooked the
alienation, disengagement
and bullying that
characterised huge schools.

get only one chance at their youth it has generally seemed reckless to tinker with their learning. It might seem unthinkable to wish that today's dentist practises in the same way as the one you had when you were a child, but as recently as the 1990s many wanted schools frozen in a state of familiarity that parents, and indeed grandparents, would find comforting.

But the transition to the 21st century proved to be a huge watershed. Curiously we approached the year 2000 looking backwards: at the amazing progress from mechanical to digital, from national to global, from pen to processor. With hindsight, we should have been looking forwards, because the first decade of the 21st century is already nurturing a revolution in our economic, social, cultural and learning lives. That revolution has such profound implications that not all of the major institutions of 20th-century learning are likely to survive.

In the last century, by and large, we built big things that did things for people – a rail service, the BBC, a national curriculum, and so on. This could be interpreted in many ways, from a pragmatic response to the postwar baby boom years, to ideological and economic determinism. The economic mantras of the last century focused on the new economics of mass production, which reached out for economies of scale (often delivered through geographical proximity). Thus we built big factories, big housing estates, big new towns, big shopping centres, huge corporations and worryingly oversized schools. Indeed the UK rewarded headteachers by paying them on a scale related not to performance but to scale: if a headteacher took a successful small school and grew it into a failing huge one, we rewarded the effort with a substantial salary rise. Big was beautiful, and the realities of mass production arguably clouded judgement on more social matters so that we overlooked the alienation, disengagement and bullying that characterised huge schools.

The closure of small schools was often justified by the rigidity of a timetable seemingly inspired by the time-and-motion clipboards of factory inspectors. "With your limited timetable," the argument

went, "you will not be able to offer Russian as a 14–18 specialism."
The huge-school timetable, like so much else that was done
organisationally for convenience rather than to engender great
learning, was one of many factors that were failing learners and
learning. But rather than ditching the rigidity and
compartmentalism of the timetable, it was always the small school
that felt the axe.

And thus the nation blundered into the barren 'cell and bell' era,
which we are struggling even now to escape. For certain, history
will show the period 1950–2000 as the era of aberration. Some
(Bowles and Gintis, 1976) have suggested a mechanistic link between
mass-production factories and the mind-deadening structures of
late 20th-century schooling. With mindless jobs to fill, and barely
7 per cent going on to university, the last thing the economy needed,
arguably, was enquiring minds. But these dull structures might
equally be seen as a simple panic engendered by the vast numbers of
postwar babies in the big developed economies. In the UK, with a
birth rate that finally peaked in 1964, at some points in the 1970s
new schools were opening every day. That speed of development
inevitably left little space for reflection, evolution or, indeed,
common sense.

How is today different? A fundamental change is that in the 21st
century new information and communications technologies have
empowered people, given them a voice and, perhaps even more
profoundly, created an era where all the success stories are about
helping people to help themselves – as seen with Google, eBay,
YouTube, Facebook and indeed with a substantial growth in the
voluntary sector too. It is a time for collegiality, collaborative
endeavour and communication. Whole industries (like travel agents)
are being passed by as people use the newly democratising tools
available to build the product that they want, on their terms.
Perfect competition, so long just a model in economics textbooks,
with buyers and sellers all knowing about each other, looks
suspiciously like eBay.

The old 'cell and bell' schools were built for a variety of reasons, none of which included being ambitious for the learners within them. Excellence came to be represented solely by the ability to conform – a huge part of teachers' days were spent imposing conformity, from examination answers to dress code, with a few perhaps tempting learners with an occasional illicit glimpse of a world of more ambitious learning: "I shouldn't tell you this until A level, but I'll tell you now anyway." If you were educated in this era, these are the teachers you remember.

Mercifully, that was then, and this is now. Today, companies look for ingenuity, for teamwork, for leadership yes, but for 'followship' too as rigid corporate hierarchies give way to more organic project-based work. They seek an ongoing commitment to learning, to exploration and to an agility of mind and practice. Rather than uniformity, employers seek that 'spark' of originality that makes a candidate stand out at interview, together with a track record of passion for learning and evidence of fitting in with others.

A tide is running across the education systems of the world: from one size fits all to personalisation; from quality control to quality assurance; from fixed short periods of timetabled learning to longer open-ended blocks, sometimes weeks long; from narrow (and often artificially distinct) subjects to project-based multidisciplinary work; from a start time at 09.00 and a finish time of 15.30 to extended opening and 24/7, 365-day access; from children ghettoised by their birthdays lying between two Septembers to mixed-age, cross-phase learning; from national to global; and so on.

All these changes have a profound influence on the physical and organisational design of education. For example, many secondary-age schools have armed some of their more turbulent children with stopwatches, telling them to record how long it takes them to finish one lesson and start another. It would be a rare school that found it was not losing 20 per cent of its learning time. In the 21st century we cannot afford to sacrifice the equivalent of Friday every week to systems that serve no purpose. More enlightened schools have abandoned the 'cells and bells' model. One by-product of this is a loss of the friction that occurred in school corridors, but the main impact is that schools being built today simply don't need corridors, because the children stay put with their heads down, learning, for much longer. And not surprisingly the considerable extra space and time thus liberated both contribute to much better engagement and performance.

Although there is a lot more to 21st-century learning spaces than simply a lack of corridors, corridors do provide a useful metaphor for the limiting and linear model of 20th-century education. Corridors slow, constrain, direct and box in. The 20th-century factory schools at their worst did the same to children's learning. Why on Earth did schools put 30 children in a room simply because they were born between two Septembers? How did they contrive to create a glut of biologists and technologists but a national shortage of biotechnologists because subjects had been compartmentalised? Why did schools imagine that they could ring a bell at 12.30 and have 1000 teenagers simultaneously hungry? Even Skinner couldn't get his rats to conform so uniformly. By limiting learning options, these factory schools were driving children's ambitions down a 'closed corridor', where success was defined in a very limited way: exam passes, linear notation, recall and conformity.

But where, in the 20th century, we had countless mindless jobs and too many children passing through schools, today we have robots to do the mindless tasks and we need ingenious engaged children to design better robots. Meanwhile, children have become scarce in western Europe and will become more so. Politically, this has moved the rhetoric away from simply 'processing' children towards a vocabulary of personalisation, of Every Child Matters and of lifelong learning. Personalisation is about being ambitious for every learner. Learners' needs change, their learning preferences change and can change daily. They even vary with the weather. Personalisation is about building learning experiences that are seductive, engaging, delightful and personal – emphatically not individualised learning (the dreaded 'drill and kill' of Bush's failing 'No child left behind'). Most of all it is full of mutuality, collegiality and helping people to help themselves: mentoring, coaching, supporting, twinning, blogging, podcasting, sharing, learning. Unsurprisingly, the physical buildings needed for a personalised education system are very different from those needed before.

Powerful technology enabled us to decode the human genome. Tomorrow's computers will be vastly more powerful yet. What will be the ambitious tasks that we might strive for and what capabilities will our learners need to be evolving today in our schools to prepare them for those tasks? Moore's Law gives us a sense of the pace of growth of microprocessor capability; perhaps we need a Heppell's Law to suggest that if learning opportunities don't keep pace with that power then we will have missed the opportunity to harness it! A significant part of that change must lie in the buildings and organisation that shape education worldwide.

Another dimension of learning's change is the leap from national to global. As you read this, consider: your shoes were made in, say, Italy, your clothes in China, your computer assembled in Ireland from components sourced in South-east Asia and designed in California. In this joined-up global world of overlapping functionality it makes absolutely no sense to talk of a 'national curriculum'. In 2007, a tiny school with five students on Little Cayman in the Caribbean joined up, through a simple IP chat facility, to an equally tiny school for older children with hemiplegia in Surrey, England. They swapped thoughts, dreams and data. The special school older children are mentoring the younger Caribbean children. It is one of many visions of the power of global learning. Be aware that neither school has even six students, yet the richness of their exchanges shows, as many have shown before, the value added from global learning interchanges.

Trying to box each end of this powerful social interaction into a different national curriculum in each of two different countries makes no sense at all. With the larger numbers we now have migrating across traditional geographical boundaries, a more global palette of learning would seem simply common sense if we are achieve the best potential for all our scarce learners. Indeed, 21st-century learning is already global in the forums and self-help communities of the internet. It is time that schools were too.

So, despite the inertia of education systems and policy, learning is changing and in some cases taking sections of formal education right along with it. Self-evidently, the conservative pace of change of educational policy is not rapid enough for that policy to be able to tell schools and learners what to do. YouTube went from start-up to billion-euro acquisition in less time than it took to develop an advisory policy about its use in schools. Policy makers have a central role, but it is of defining vision and philosophy and then asking schools and learners how to achieve that vision effectively. This is the reality of the bottom-up world of new learning. But around the world schools and learners are not prepared to wait, or to power down to enter education; they are getting on themselves with some remarkable changes, armed with powerful technology in their pockets and desks, linked to reassuring pioneers worldwide, and buoyed up by exceptional results. The revolution that is 21st-century learning, and the radical spaces that are evolving to house it, are both unstoppable. The only two questions left are whether these new learning spaces will be schools in any sense, and just how good our learners might be if together we get the designs right.

It's shaping up to be quite a century already.

www.heppell.net

Bibliography
Bowles S, Gintis H. Schooling in Capitalist America: Educational reform and the contradictions of economic life. New York: Basic Books; 1976.

Dramatic clinical spaces

Anthony Pinching
Jeff Teare
Simon Turley

A playwright, a theatre director and a clinician-scientist, all of them active as educators as well as practitioners, have forged an enduring working relationship. First coming together to develop a play examining the impact of HIV/AIDS, the relationship has blossomed into an ongoing collaboration. Here, *Anthony Pinching*, *Jeff Teare* and *Simon Turley* reflect on the personal journeys they have undertaken as they have explored each other's professional and cultural space – and how the journey has enabled them to gain greater insight into themselves and their work.

Stated simply, we have been developing plays about HIV and about chronic fatigue syndrome (CFS/ME). While these stand as entities and performances, the ideas, situations and contexts have also been developed in workshops with young people at school, medical students, health professionals and patients. As a team from varied disciplines working on the Theatrescience project, we have engaged in dialogues and discourses that have increasingly taken us from fairly straightforward issues of securing veracity towards establishing a deeper and wider authenticity. This journey should give us, and others, greater insights into the interfaces between our humanity/identity and the processes through which we explore outer and inner worlds.

As individuals, each of us has multiple perspectives and formal professional spaces – e.g. teacher and playwright, theatre director and educator, clinician and scientist. But the richness of teamwork has been about discovering each other's spaces, and creatively working within and across them. This has taken time (and several plays). Respect for the expertise and experience in those other spaces has been interlaced with a guided exploration of each other's domains. This reached a point where we could, albeit briefly, even consider changing places.

For art to inform science, for drama to reveal the person behind the illness, for the learner to experience the space of another person, for the (trainee) clinician to comprehend the vulnerability of the patient, for the well person to know disease, for the ill person to see other ways of being, we may need similarly to exchange roles,

to witness or act out our incomprehension. We have developed
these issues especially in dramas about CFS/ME, where major
biomedical uncertainties are embodied in pervasive illness with
a life-changing impact.

Perhaps in leaving behind caricature views of the spaces that we
occupy in our various roles, we can identify a new intermediate
space that allows us to give expression to those vital aspects of
ourselves that cannot be expressed within narrowly defined roles.

Theatre, science and space – a history

In 2001–02, Jeff Teare and Rebecca Gould, co-directors of
Tinderbox Consultants Limited, worked on Science Centrestage
– the Wellcome Trust's flagship Year of Science project, which
involved 93 schools creating pieces of drama based on
biomedical science – followed in 2003 by the Newbury and
Plymouth Science/Drama Festivals, involving 12 schools.

Imagining the Future followed, an exploratory creative project
combining scientists, writers, actors and directors. One of
the writers was Simon Turley and several scientists came from
the Peninsula Medical School. Jeff then developed the Drama
of Science project, introducing teachers and educationalists in
five major cities to the use of drama to explore biomedical
science issues.

The next evolutionary step was Theatre of Science, a large-scale
project at the Theatre Royal Plymouth (2004–05), involving
projects by 16 schools and three community groups, as well as
two professional productions. One of these productions was
Seeing Without Light (published by Parthian, 2005) examining
themes around HIV research, written by Simon, directed by Jeff,
with Professor Anthony Pinching from the Peninsula Medical
School as scientific adviser.

From this collaboration came a new script about CFS/ME, called *Sleeping Beauties*. This script was developed by Simon, Tony and Jeff for Tinderbox, now operating under the name of Theatrescience[1]. Scenes from *Sleeping Beauties* were presented at three conferences, and the whole script was read at the Royal Academy of Dramatic Arts (RADA). This work was funded by a Wellcome Trust People Award; it was externally evaluated by Mel Scaffold, and quotations from this are included within this article by her kind agreement.

Sleeping Beauties has subsequently transmogrified into a different play about CFS/ME, now called *Something Somatic*. This play also received a public reading at RADA. *Something Somatic* was first performed in late 2007.

Simon Turley: A rude awakening for beauty

When it came to science, I thought I was an empty space: content- and value-free. But of course that wasn't true. I knew one or two things about genes – an admittedly dilatory biology O level ensured that once I had had to know something about genes. And Jeff Teare's brilliantly apt, oft-repeated initial Theatrescience workshop exercise, where all those assembled create an instant image of themselves – first as scientists and then as artists – showed that my value system was firmly stuck in the tradition of the two cultures: my scientist focused, my artist fey. Imagining the Future started something quite profound for me. By the end of that week, which brought writers into direct contact with science and scientists, my supposed space had been delineated, questioned and broken open…into a bigger space. When Jeff presented a series of potential scenarios for plays about biomedical issues, I stepped firmly through: I was going to write a play that would be about both finding a 'gene therapy' for HIV/AIDS and the relationship between science and art.

Drafts of *Seeing Without Light* were generously informed and scrutinised by several scientists, including Tony Pinching, who joined the Peninsula Medical School during the development. By the time we met, Tony had read the current draft and was encouraging – alive to what I was trying to do with the bigger (theatre-metaphor) picture. He also had a veracity-spanner or two to throw into the mix. My concept of genetic immunity to HIV, a central plot point, was at best confused and at worst just wrong. He outlined alternative scenarios of immunity and helped me towards a new and pleasing shape for the story. Tony also shared his experience of working in sub-Saharan Africa (parts of the play are set in Kenya), and we even explored moving a substantial part of the Kenyan character's story to London.

Tony was thus sharing a creative space not only with me, the writer, but also with Jeff, who was my dramaturge throughout the project. When the play was in production, the three of us shared the stage (a space to which we had all contributed, but which we now occupied together) for post-show discussions. In response to a question about the project, Tony said that what each of us was doing in our different fields was "trying to make a bit more sense of the world". For me, this was a moment that defined Theatrescience.

I later attended Tony's inaugural Peninsula Medical School lecture, 'Journeys with Patients'. I was expecting to be informed, but I had not anticipated being moved. However, lectures happen in lecture 'theatres', so maybe I should have been better prepared. His accounts of working with people suffering from HIV/AIDS and CFS/ME were unfailingly humane. It was clearly there in his voice, as he recalled a man with HIV/AIDS gently refusing Tony's latest range of strategies for managing his condition with an acceptance that it was "time to go". In the audience, what I heard was not science but grief – I found that I had held my breath until he resumed speaking. Tony's metaphor of the clinician as mountain-guide, attending patients on their journey through illness, reinforced for me the notion of the doctor as a human being first, and a scientist second. His observation that sometimes in the consulting room he had become aware of a third presence, alongside the clinician and the patient – that presence being the disease itself – was to stay with me.

In an illness like CFS/ME, there's a considerable gap where scientific certainty might be expected to be found, a space where, in Tony's words, it is "the art of medicine" which must be practised. My subsequent suggestion to Tony that there was a play in CFS/ME, and that he might like to write it, seemed logical enough. While gently demurring at my suggestion, he contended that there were "several plays" to be written about the disease.

We immediately turned to Jeff, who conjured funding and generated the essential energy to form a project. The three of us were increasingly aware that CFS/ME provided, above all, a dramatic setting where we were not dealing with the emerging social impact of scientific certainties, but a profound disease reality that lacked a secure biomedical science construct, giving double jeopardy to those affected. The theatre provided a natural space to explore the actual human experience, grounded in personhood, without requiring first the secure anchorage of – as yet limited – scientific knowledge. On the other hand, Tony was always keen to underpin the emerging drama with clinical insights and a coherent hypothetical scientific framework.

We co-opted two young actors and a rehearsal room, where through discussion and improvisation we began to form some shapes for a play. Tony's contacts with the CFS/ME communities allowed Jeff and me to start a more detailed research process. Quite early on I had formed the idea of the sufferer as a sleeping-beauty figure: an archetype of passive and arrested humanity – an innocent, a victim – their life on hold, waiting to be released by the right prince delivering the right kiss. Repeatedly, in the accounts of the disease that we heard, there was confirmation of this. Indeed,

the parents of one particularly severely afflicted sufferer told us that her occupational therapist referred to her as "my sleeping beauty".

Research sprawls, but a play must be a concentration of something. Tony's words that there were several plays in CFS/ME came back to haunt me. We were never likely to attract sufficient funding to produce an epic play with a large cast. However, if this piece were to be about one sufferer, what should be the age, the ethnicity, the socioeconomic status and the gender? No sooner had I made one choice than the stories I was therefore excluding clamoured ever louder for my attention, while the one I *had* corralled seemed to shrink.

Tony, at Jeff's suggestion, mapped a clinical path for an archetypal CFS/ME sufferer; it put an order to her symptoms and her encounters with her GP and then a succession of consultants, who would subsequently find that she did not have a disease in their field. This document, which Jeff calls "the stations of the cross", then became the engine for my various plays under the title *Sleeping Beauties*. I made the CFS/ME sufferer a school student and then a woman in her 30s. I then created a play in which these two characters are subsumed into one (played by two actors). I put doctors into the play, then removed them and experimented with trying to transform the audience into the listening clinician. I anthropomorphised CFS/ME as an invasive, cocky male character.

Good actors were worked hard by Jeff and delivered the play truthfully (in rehearsed-reading form) at conferences of medical professionals, of CFS/ME community groups, and in theatre spaces. Responses were mixed. *Sleeping Beauties* seemed to have potential as a piece of applied drama – it could inform audiences, it could raise questions about clinical practice. Health professionals and students valued it as a way of enhancing their own training; it could build awareness of the human dimensions of an illness, where the very uncertainty can be felt as a threat to their role. Patients and CFS/ME

Left:
Rachel Donovan as Emma
in *Something Somatic*.
Miriam Nabarro

community groups were pleased to see their hitherto ignored realities revealed so publicly, were moved to see their own experiences transplanted to the theatre space, and were impressed at the absorption of their personal experiences into a singular storyline.

However, I had failed to create a play that excited me as a piece of theatre. And I watched, appalled but somehow not over-surprised, as, during a full reading of the play, a theatre professional – whose partner, an actor, was reading a major role – nodded off...this was a sleeping beauty too far. While Jeff and Rebecca Gould pursued production funding for the project, I fretted...and, eventually, started over again.

In *Something Somatic*, the audience finds itself sharing the theatre space with a naked actor. It witnesses a relationship between the character he plays and Emma, a young, successful, but increasingly ill woman. It watches as he insinuates his way into her life. Emma finds him some clothing, and he systematically reorders and then, apparently randomly, destroys her flat. There is no explicit mention of CFS/ME, and only an emerging sense that the action of the play is not actually happening in the space that is being presented at all.

I have narrowed the focus in this new play. It is a more intense concentration of something. And, while the breadth of our researches may not be represented in the plot, I believe that a bigger story is emerging, about the relationship all of us have with our bodies, their innate fragility, and their uninvited guests. Emma's flat becomes a theatre-metaphor for her body: its systems progressively malfunctioning, so that rather than being a place of ultimate refuge, it becomes a prison of discomforts.

This play started its life in Tony's inaugural lecture, where human narratives in the clinical setting seemed to be requiring another wider space. It has moved through workshop spaces, where it has served rather utilitarian functions in education and training, and had undoubted value. It has finally returned to the theatre, where other audiences will experience *Something Somatic*. I am confident that none of them will be dozing off.

Jeff Teare: My life in sciart

In 2001 I first got involved in biomedical science-based drama/theatre, as a somewhat veteran theatre director without a science qualification, but experience of directing over 100 productions, ranging from Shakespeare to puppets for the under-fives; only one of these had been in any way 'about' science. My peers had got into the sometimes gruelling world of medical role-play (48 versions of 'breaking the bad news' in one day?!) but their experience of the efficacy of such work varied. Otherwise 'science' was a 'space' that I did not visit.

Much of my theatre work had been about comparative storytelling (folk tales, myths etc.) and sociopolitical issues, and most of my biomedical science-based drama (accent on the participation) and theatre (accent on the performance/audience) in the last six years has used story (comparative or otherwise) in a sociopolitical context. I realised that the scientific method (roughly: idea–theory–test–confirm or change idea/theory–test again–publish) is not so far from what happens in rehearsing a play (idea–script–rehearsal–confirm or change idea/script–rehearse again–perform).

In joining Imagining the Future, experience in community-based theatre led me to want to engage with a local writer and, given the nature of the project, Simon as a writer who was also a teacher seemed ideal. The Peninsula Medical School was one of our partners on the Theatre of Science project and Tony – given his expertise in HIV/AIDS, as both clinician and scientist – soon came on board Theatre of Science as scientific adviser on Simon's play *Seeing Without Light*.

Top:
Theatrescience workshop
in India.

Bottom:
Theatrescience Bangalore
Festival participants.

A Pinching, J Teare, S Turley

Very quickly it became obvious that Tony wasn't inclined to limit his input to the entirely scientific and technical; he had artistic ideas too. Simon politely draws the line when I get carried away with my own writing ideas. They sometimes listen when I suggest how the work might actually be applied in a theatre. Slowly the three of us have begun to develop a properly creative relationship.

In delivering a drama special study unit at the School, using drama to explore personal attitudes to the 'art' as opposed to the science of medicine, it soon became clear that the personal spaces that the medical students and I filled were not that different. Is CFS/ME a physiological disorder or is it psychological ('all-in-the-mind'), or is it both? I have to 'cope', why can't 'they'? These are thoughts that we all had, and they needed to be expressed and explored in order that they could be honestly addressed. Drama enables expression without immediate embarrassment or guilt. The 'space' that drama creates, at its best, enables both honest debate and potential movement.

This is especially true in schools. I have seen students' eyes open and opinions change, having engaged with dramatic character and situation. I've also seen them learn some science in the drama studio – although that, for me at least, was never really the point. The evaluation of our project identified a correlation between a better understanding of the personal and social impact of CFS/ME and more positive attitudes. Responses from students confirmed the potential of drama as a way of learning that offers an alternative to traditional pedagogical methods in exploring both the condition and clinician–patient communication. Thinking about biomedical science is thinking about society, ethics, economics and politics – it's as simple as that.

Another interesting space is the swish bar at the Royal Academy of Dramatic Arts. It's here, as part of their extracurricular programme, that we've done public readings (very mixed audiences) of our three scripts, followed by discussion. Although questionnaires provided some formal evaluations, the discussions ensured that the work really did get 'tested' by actors and audiences, and changed.

Some six years on from my first dabblings, I find myself in quite a different 'space'. Running workshops to find ways to dramatise such characters as DNA, ATP, HIV and, of course, the essentially dramatic CFS. But, if there's anything I've learnt from our collaboration so far, it's that there's not much in life that isn't about science somehow, and that we're all capable of art, even if only in our dreams.

Anthony Pinching: Journeys in drama

As a clinician, I need to be able to inhabit, comprehend, interpret, heal and restore other people's internal spaces, as people, and as altered by the experience of illness. Active listening and the performative use of verbal and non-verbal communication are crucial tools; narrative and metaphor are essential ingredients in clinical discourse.

My experience in drama has been very much as an amateur (acting, lighting), but has also included work, as a clinical specialist, with the Royal Court Theatre and others on the use of drama and drama workshops to explore and project around HIV and AIDS, during the early years.

When I was invited to collaborate with Simon and Jeff on *Seeing Without Light*, there was initially a straightforward task of checking the script scientifically and clinically for credibility and veracity. The drama was already very well conceptualised and substantially developed. It explored several areas, including innate resistance to HIV or AIDS, and cultural collisions between Africa and the West, between clinical need and scientific imperatives, between the studier and the studied, and between art and science.

However, I needed to help Simon resolve the important biological and conceptual distinction between resistance to HIV infection on the one hand, and resistance to AIDS in someone with HIV on the other, which had become conflated. Breaking this, gently but firmly, to Simon at our first encounter could have been the end of our work together! But instead it began our fascinating voyage together – and later with Jeff as director – exploring our conceptual and technical expert spaces.

Initially, I just outlined in plain language the two sorts of resistance, illustrated by examples from clinical experience and scientific literature. We were soon embedded in personal narratives from my clinical work (which I always draw upon), as well as from wider social dimensions here and in Africa. Simon showed an uncanny ability to absorb and then re-present material from our conversations, conceptually or literally, within the script. He readily incorporated the technical corrections, indeed capitalising upon them.

During rehearsals, I enjoyed conveying to the team some unique human experiences I had had as a clinical scientist, working on HIV/AIDS during the 1980s, much of which related to the roles displayed. The performances transformed my own views, through their different perspectives. Although I had provided some of the raw materials, the drama was different again – deployed by new characters in a theatre space that required a different kind of attention. The dramatic setting created a new distance for perspective, and a new proximity of experience, unlinked from my particulars.

Post-show discussions were fascinating, drawing out fresh insights, not least due to the varied backgrounds of audience members, including school kids who had been doing their own workshops. The children had a freshness and clarity of perspective that, as ever, avoided the encumbrance of baggage that adults tend to stack up, obscuring the essence. Their probing 'whys' showed that the workshops had already taken them on quite a journey.

Finally, I also discovered, sitting on stage answering questions with the production team, that I now occupied part of their space.

Shortly after, I gave my inaugural lecture at Peninsula – 'Journeys with Patients' – to which Simon came. In a previous inaugural I had covered my scientific development. Here I explored the art of medicine, learnt (as with much of the science) from patients throughout my career. I illustrated it not with PowerPoint but with themed narratives, most from patients with HIV/AIDS or CFS/ME. Afterwards, Simon asked: "Why don't we do a play on CFS/ME?" To which the only possible reply was: "When shall we start?"

We met to draw together our strands of thought and expertise at a happily named hostelry, The Weavers. We saw how many issues could valuably be explored about CFS/ME through drama. I was taken aback, but pleasurably, when Simon asked if I wanted to write the play, apparently because of my use of narrative, but we soon got back into our respective expert spaces. The exchange revealed the extent to which we were creatively crossing boundaries.

I started to see how drama could convey the human experience of this horrible illness to people who found it hard to relate to or conceptualise. The narrative of characters, with whom they could relate, would root their reactions into personal space, rather than being set into the amorphous and anonymous limbo created by phrases such as 'an illness of unknown cause' or biopsychosocial disease models. Clinicians, students, the wider public, patients and carers would all likely gain from the revelatory human dimensions in drama. We ranged over stories and issues, peppered with examples from recent patients. I later saw ideas and even phrases reappearing in scripts, alongside insights from many others, through Simon's uncanny ability to absorb, incorporate and deploy.

A two-day workshop with Jeff, Simon and two actors was extraordinary in the speed with which dramatic representation of daily clinical experiences gained fresh life. Two minutes of drama could convey more than hours of lectures! We started with accounts of our own experiences of health problems. The actors read a brief factual account of CFS/ME, interspersed with comments from me about how this felt. By lunchtime, the actors, under Jeff's deft guidance, were revealing in short improvisations how drama could make visible this painfully invisible illness and its human costs. I felt able to suggest not just how the illness might affect how a person might move, but also how different people would react, and be differently moved.

Simon and Jeff met up with many patients, carers and clinicians. Fragments of a play were then presented at meetings. The impact was, as expected, very strong. An experienced clinician and a CFS researcher were both convinced they recognised the patient, although neither had met the (composite) patient. They were equally compelled by the idea of the illness as an additional character in the patient's life. Clinicians valued the opportunity to see the human dramas within the 'patient' and among those around. After another performance, an uncharacteristic initial silence from patient advocates was later explained as choking from seeing their own experiences so closely re-created. Veracity and authenticity were being established.

Building sessions with fragments of the play into conferences always introduced an element of surprise, with a frame-shift from formal abstractions to human experience. Clinical audiences initially focused on the 'how to do it' (the clinical role), while patients were more struck by the 'how it felt' (the illness experience). Yet all reflected later how portrayal through dramatic space had changed their perspectives, creating different alliances and seeing themselves better in context. Patients could benefit by being able to see similar experiences at a distance, enabling them to reinterpret their own reactions, without being directly challenged. I even thought of having actors performing brief scenes in patients' homes, as musicians have, bringing the theatre's metaphorical space as a guest into their own personal spaces.

When readings of *Sleeping Beauties* took place at the Royal Academy of Dramatic Arts and the Barbican Theatre in Plymouth, the portrayal of the diverse human responses to the illness was strongly resonant with what I heard in clinics, and the characters (including the two versions of the affected patient) had preternatural clarity. Audience responses, including from those who had no personal knowledge of the illness, revealed the potency of drama in conveying it.

The external evaluation confirmed that CFS/ME was seen as a suitable topic for theatre and art to engage with:

> [The positive response from audiences] indicates not only the aptness of theatre as a means of conveying information, but also suggests that theatre is not merely a tool for making biomedicine accessible – through 'theatre in education' – but benefits positively from the relationship in gaining a new subject for art in its own right.
> ...
> Theatre may be effective in this context because of the humanisation of the condition, the delineation and exploration of something that becomes more than a set of symptoms, but begins to show societal impact (the effect on the sufferer's relationships) as well as the personal experience (of the physical effects, of communication with medical professionals and the journey to diagnosis and beyond).

The evaluation also highlighted some of the reasons why the play had managed to achieve its impact:

The script was effective in conveying an experience, not simply because it was translating that experience into drama, but also because of the style of the piece; the contrast between the humour of much of the dialogue and the gravity of the sufferer's condition. One audience member commented: 'Light-hearted comedy helped engage with text. Serious moments were therefore heightened – they conveyed a message'.

Feedback from medical students doing medical humanities theatre workshops with Jeff (three sessions and a performance, spread through the fourth year) showed they had gained deep insights into the human responses to CFS/ME. They also recognised the potency of the clinician's response to the patient's illness in affecting outcomes and attitudes – positively or negatively – as well as gaining more true understanding of the illness than from lectures or reading. The shift of space and mode enabled a quite different education. This point was also drawn out in the evaluation:

Students scored the efficacy of drama in exploring CFS/ME very highly:

> [they] were very positive about the learning methods they used on this course. A [similarly high] score…was recorded when students were questioned about their opinion of drama as a way of exploring medical communication…supported by students' comments during the post-reading discussion.…One participant said she had found it very useful to evaluate the way she communicates: 'You realise phrases that sound sympathetic in your head are inappropriate'.

Key to this self-discovery was the safe environment in which students could experiment with ways of communicating, by adopting personas and speaking 'in character'. Despite the novelty of the approach, students found it a rewarding experience:

...students scored their enjoyment of the course very highly... supported by several comments about the nature of the teaching style: 'fun', 'an alternative and enjoyable way to learn about a medical condition' and 'a chance to be creative' typify the positive responses. Only one student responded negatively to the teaching methods....the drama exercises...'took me outside of my comfort zone'. Despite this, he recorded a [high] score... when asked about the extent to which the SSU [special study unit] had contributed to his understanding of CFS/ME.

The Medical Humanities programme at the Peninsula Medical School, of which this drama SSU is a part, integrates the art of medicine with the science, to enhance students' sensibility to patients' lives and experiences. The success of this SSU has shown not only the value of the different learning experience, but has also enabled students to acquire fresh insights into the perspectives of patients with an illness surrounded by so much uncertainty and stigma.

Later, while discussing this chapter, Simon let slip that he had moved on from *Sleeping Beauties*, and was writing an entirely different play, although retaining the character of the illness. The shock to me was palpable, and persisted through reading the new script of *Something Somatic* (with a much subtler way of revealing CFS/ME). I wanted to discuss how to retain the earlier entity in some way. There may have been a utilitarian element, having seen its value for professionals and patients, but I think I was actually experiencing loss – of our offspring, and the dramatic representation of a shared witness to this illness.

Here was an intriguing mix of role shifts, which I haven't yet fully disentangled. Rationally, I could see that, as a drama, the new play was stronger, with more implicit, almost glancing, insights into the impact of CFS/ME. Yet emotionally, I had just witnessed the slaying by the author of a familiar and important, if rather dysfunctional, family! Upset? Me, the clinician who usually manages other people's real losses? Talk about occupying the spaces of others!

As we move towards production – and the release of both scripts – I find myself eagerly anticipating that it may enable the wider public to comprehend better the impact of this illness and to respond more supportively to those affected.

As we have outlined in our proposals for funding of this project – in the domain of increasing public engagement with science and medicine – there is perhaps more complexity, as well as a greater need to depict the impact of an illness that is characterised by its invisibility and its (current) lack of an established biomedical explanation. We have benefited from a genuinely creative tension as we have attempted both to depict an illness and reveal the experience of illness.

The dramatic art in *Something Somatic* may not give us all the answers, but it certainly helps us ask better questions. Just like scientific research really...

1 www.theatrescience.org.uk

Visiting Time and *Boychild*: site-specific pedagogical experiments on the boundaries of theatre and science

Anna Ledgard

What happens when science education and theatre vacate their traditional domains, the classroom and the theatre? *Anna Ledgard* has been intimately involved in two innovative projects that have taken participants into some highly unlikely spaces – including performances in a working hospital and a deserted former military installation. The learning experience associated with such projects is undeniably richer but may be challenging to fully describe – or assess.

It was Oscar Wilde who said:

> I regard the theatre as the greatest of all art forms, the most immediate way in which a human being can share with another the sense of what it is to be a human being.

If we are to engage the next generation of students in science learning then the ways in which science concepts are introduced need to acknowledge the role of science in human affairs and be relevant to our lives as lived. It could be argued, then, that the use of theatre as a means of exploring the role of science in everyday lives can deepen insights into the human condition and create powerful new forms of arts and science learning. Such experiments require us to stretch the boundaries of conventional science teaching or theatre practice, taking activities beyond the physical spaces of school or classroom, theatre or studio, and opening up new spaces for learning.

The two projects I shall explore in this chapter, *Visiting Time* and *Boychild*, were developed and performed in spaces and places not dedicated to performance ends and had as their goal the engagement of communities in science learning. Both projects involved adults and children in an extended interdisciplinary arts process and innovative live performances, providing an experimental conceptual 'space' for learning. The work took place in a variety of physical places and spaces, some dedicated education spaces, others sites or settings offering a range of resources and opportunities.

Artists and theatre makers, like scientists, are driven by a deep curiosity and an urge to find out what makes the world tick; for them the drama process is the laboratory for their experiments. But working outside the narrow disciplinary framework that science teaching sometimes imposes, the artist is free to investigate scientific knowledge in the broader context of human lives and concerns. Artists can work outside the conventions that tend to separate minds from bodies, thoughts from feelings, and medical knowledge from patients' lived experience.

Boychild and *Visiting Time* were experiments in this hybrid world. They provided opportunities for students to explore the ways in which science applies to the world and to human experience, personal lives and communities. The experiments raise important questions not only about arts and science learning, and the spaces and places in which it takes place, but perhaps even more importantly, about learning itself.

This chapter is an attempt to explore the underlying principles behind these two experiments and their wider educational impact. How do we ensure that our work is good art and genuinely innovative as well as meeting educational objectives? How do we find a language to articulate arts and science learning? How do we balance arts making with the priorities of education institutions and curricula? How do we balance open-ended exploration with the need to inform?

The projects

Visiting Time and *Boychild* were collaborations between West Dorset General Hospitals NHS Trust and education organisations in West Dorset, and were funded by Arts Council England and the Wellcome Trust. They both involved me as educationalist and producer, and the artist Mark Storor in a distinctive style of participatory performance practice leading to site-specific performances.

Storor's unique approach to interdisciplinary arts practice clearly had a profound impact on participants and was perceived as genuinely innovative by many of its reviewers and audiences. It is of course impossible to do full justice to the magic and sheer 'live-ness' of these events in words on a page. Andrew Whittuck and Robert Quincey's compelling images, and the poetry that accompanied *Visiting Time* and *Boychild* from the beginning, have assisted me greatly in bringing an extra dimension to this description.

In 2004 *Visiting Time* opened in the East Wing of Dorset County Hospital, with audiences of five at a time invited to an 'appointment' for 'treatment'. They were tagged and swabbed, and led by performers, all clad in pyjamas and pillow-head masks, through a working hospital, encountering along the way a series of performance installations. In one a 'pillow-head' figure, limbless, trapped in a cotton-wool cocoon, attempted to keep a balloon in the air (see image, right). In the lecture theatre a scientist asked the audience the enigmatic question: "How can I make a snowball when my hands are always hot?", referring to a condition associated with cystic fibrosis.

Above:
Visiting Time, Dorset County Hospital, 2004.
Andrew Whittuck

Visiting Time came out of a collaboration between West Dorset General Hospitals NHS Trust and the Sir John Colfox School, Bridport. The piece was devised with help from a young patient with cystic fibrosis, hospital staff, nurses and a geneticist. Its substantive thematic content was to investigate the science and human impact of genetic inheritance, but aesthetically the task was about the possibilities of making performance in spaces not dedicated to performance ends, in this case a working hospital.

Theatre has for some time been experimenting with the relationship between spectators and participants by drawing audiences physically into the mechanics of the setting, thereby eroding the separation of audience and performance.

Visiting Time's tagging of its audience as 'patients' similarly dissolved these boundaries but also identified the 'spectators' as individual human beings, albeit as processed by a medical bureaucracy. Their presence in a working hospital alongside 'real' patients added further impact.

The first public performance of *Boychild* took place on Father's Day, 17 June 2007, in a defunct wing of the former Admiralty Underwater Weapons Establishment at Portland, Dorset. Audiences, ten at a time, were led on an archetypal journey through the life of a male from birth to old age. The performance integrated scientific knowledge with glimpses of the memories, fears, desires and thoughts of men and boys towards maleness in society today, gathered during the preceding 12 months. The participants were over 80 boys and men aged from infancy to old age (in schools, a young offenders institution, with artists and scientists, fathers, fathers-to-be and elderly men in working men's clubs).

Boychild

An older man, 70, loses the thread. As his thoughts unravel, his mind elsewhere, an alarm goes off. Boychild, 7 opens a door and leads us out of confusion.

Boychild, 21, a fetus suspended in a tank, contemplates the father he is yet to meet. He wonders if his-story will repeat itself.

Overwhelmed by a kaleidoscopic plethora of conflicting and ever-erupting feelings, it is a tricky business, navigating one's way through the turbulent emotional landscape inhabited by Boychild, 7.

His body, an oddly shaped potato, with unfamiliar sproutings, torments. Neither man nor...Boychild, 14, struggles to come to terms with the inevitable.

Endocrinologist, 39, a boychild himself, explains fetal biology.

Boychild, 35, an expectant father, sings a hymn to his unborn child.

Ensconced in a rose garden, Boychild, 70, fondly remembers. Boychild, 7 makes him a cup of tea…

Boychild, early 40s, *undertakes* the last shave. It is important he goes out as he came in.

Boychild, 21,500 ft above sea level, adorned with his grandfather's cufflinks, beckons us to the table. He donates his organs.

Transforming space: the workshop processes
In describing his work Storor makes constant reference to the way in which theatre can help to illuminate behaviours and experiences that may be deeply buried or hidden within us:

> All I'm interested in is what it is to be human and to be moved and to feel something even if you don't know what it is… (Mark Storor, interview transcript, 8 July 2007)

Storor's methodology is consistent in its starting-point: "Once I'm working with people, ethically it has to be about what those people start with." This insistence is rooted in his own strongly held pedagogy, focused on the needs of the learner. At the same time both of us are well aware of how difficult it can be to maintain such principles when working within different kinds of organisation and with multiple partners.

Drawing sensitively on the place in which the learners find themselves is a central feature of the method. For example, the preoccupation of the seven-year-olds with their feelings (both

Above:
Boychild workshop, 2007.
Andrew Whittuck

physical and emotional) led to an exploration of the biological functions of the body – the heart, the brain, the nervous system, blood vessels. In a workshop space, ribbons of different colours, representing blood vessels, the nervous system and sinews, were physically attached to the body of a child, with reference to human anatomy books (see images, left). This 'dramatisation' provided an introduction to important biological concepts. Further factual knowledge was sought in a visit to At-Bristol science centre. A workshop with science graduates offered insights into the workings of the senses. As far as the school science curriculum was concerned, important learning had been covered, but for the children their interesting quasi-philosophical question, 'How many feelings does a boy have in a day?', remained unanswered.

Storor talks of the importance of transforming space, or "transgressing it", and a feature of all his workshops is the changing of the space from "literal" to "dramatic", from "expected" to "unexpected". This is done either by removing familiar patterns and arrangements of furniture, or by bringing in symbolic objects, such as the seven sets of vests and pants, from babygro to XXXL or the seven male overcoats laid out across the floor. This serves the process well, the deliberate choices and juxtapositions of objects and colours (red plastic bowls, blue backgrounds, timeless white vests and pants, hospital-issue pyjamas) hinting at atmospheres and meanings while reconfiguring the familiar surroundings of school hall or classroom. It has the added advantage of creating an expectation or curiosity, and what Storor describes as "a disruption in the physiognomy of the people coming into the room". This "disruption" happens as the perception of space moves from literal to symbolic, having the potential to become the space for new kinds of thinking.

Nowhere was this sense of space more dramatically realised than in our work at Portland's Young Offenders Institution. Portland inscribed itself on our consciousness from day one. Our many journeys along the coastal road, the steep climb onto Portland and the stunning views back along Chesil Beach contrasted sharply with the journey through the entry cages of the prison.

The discovery of Southwell Park, the disused wing of the former Admiralty Underwater Weapons Establishment, added yet more symbolic overtones, invoking a further set of metaphors for masculinity and maleness. The building itself brought to Boychild 'representations' of working lives based in cell-like workspaces, designed for individual, isolated activity. The original centrally controlled loudspeaker system still connected corridors of numbered rooms and even extended along the once impenetrable perimeter fence. This was a building that could add its own narrative while holding the stories of boys and men without distracting from their essence (see image, right). Contrasting undercurrents of great tenderness and the potential for violence that had emerged from the artistic development process seemed almost echoed in the fabric of the building itself, as well as the placing of the images within it.

Above:
'Follow me', *Boychild*, 2007.

Andrew Whittuck

The artist's filter is perhaps at its sharpest when images and ideas from workshop processes meet the physical context for performance. Once responding to the space every choice is deliberate and nuanced and has potential to add to or distract from the existing narratives:

> ...by sharpening the aesthetic and keeping it bare you honour the story because it has nothing extraneous around it...
> (Mark Storor)

In the performance the choice to invite the smallest boys to descend the stairs, still too little to unlock the doors and let us in unaided; or the deliberate juxtaposing of repeated door-slamming with the gentleness of a small child making tea for his grandfather: these are the kind of precise decisions that permeate the performance methodology.

One of the most memorable moments of *Boychild* in the Young Offenders Institution was when the young men raced to get into a babygro (5'10" young men encased in 18-month-olds' babygros). The activity was in part a strategy to regain the energy that an intervening week in prison had dulled, and also to assist the transition from the space of prison to the imaginative space of our workshops. The initial playful game led us back to a young man's very serious question: was I born to be a criminal? The strong symbolism of the babygro – its ambivalent connections with 'innocence' – was a strong visual cue to reflection on the nurturing of 'the boy' in the often disrupted social contexts which were familiar to our group.

> My dad made me get the thing to beat me.
> Dad was discipline, judge and sentencer.
> My mum called us her pitbulls, there were nine of us,
> She was tired by the time she had me.
> (Portland Young Offenders Institution participants group poem, 2006)

Artistic practice

Storor's work defies easy definition although it has some reference points in 'live art', forum theatre and theatre-in-education, where participants engage both physically and emotionally in a deeply embodied learning process. It shares some features with applied drama. In *Applied Drama: The gift of theatre*, Helen Nicholson offers a definition:

> Applied drama is principally concerned with enabling people to move beyond the ordinary and everyday and use the aesthetics of drama, theatre and performance to gain new insights into the social and cultural practices of life. (2005, p. 129)

There are of course risks to undertaking this work. These are in part mediated by clear facilitation structures, strong partnerships and a consistent pedagogy. It is the credible 'voice' of the pedagogical and organisational framework that can enable institutions to feel safe with what might otherwise be perceived as considerable levels of risk. Artist's and producer's understanding of their ethical responsibilities is also critical (see Nicholson, 2005, pp. 155–67).

However, paying attention to the safety of the 'space' for experimentation and maintaining trusting relationships is vital to the wellbeing of all, as well as being the key to the 'truth' of the final performance. Storor engages as fully in the artistic process himself as he would expect others to. Trust was sealed early on in *Visiting Time* when he cut off his beard as his contribution to the gathering of fragments of our genetic material. Not only was this a moment of pure theatre – it set off an audible gasp among the group – it also sent a message that this work was going to require genuine commitment. It also signalled that this would be a two-way process, characterised by reciprocal relationships. Storor is emphatic that he does not separate his creative and pedagogic practice:

> There is absolutely no difference between my own creative practice and my participative practice. All I'm interested in is making art and in making the art I want to hone my own skills as an artist...actually the most important thing is to have a genuine dialogue with the person that you're working with and the place and the meeting point between the two of us is where the art happens. If you're holding back from bringing your own self into that arena then actually the work is meaningless. (Interview, 8 July 2007)

Science and theatre

Both *Visiting Time* and *Boychild* took science learning outside the classroom and involved adults and children in an extended interdisciplinary arts process and innovative live performances. Both engaged with an exploratory methodology premised on the belief that significant learning can be gained through the shared exploration of personal stories and their embodiment in site-specific performance.

The projects illustrate that theatre can in certain conditions place a screen around experience, transforming it into potent metaphors with significance and meaning for others. In the perceptive words of a student of applied theatre:

> ...real behaviour can become performance, real stories can become art and real experiences become archetypal...
> (Aylwyn Walsh, July 2007)

In *Boychild* a connection with science ran though the entire performance – sometimes only hinted at in the juxtaposition of ideas and images, like the sperm made of a lifetime's worth of human hair, or the undertaker correcting a popular misconception that hair can continue to grow after death. On occasion it was factually informative, as when an endocrinologist explains the genetic origins of the male. The opening moments of the event reference the blurring of reality of Alzheimer's disease as the soundtrack in the audience's ears becomes increasingly dislocated from the elderly man who tries to remember why he stands before them until finally his words disintegrate entirely (see image, near right).

Perhaps not surprisingly, given the ages of the schoolboys, the experience of puberty became an important theme. The difficulty of disentangling the emotional and physical was explored in their writings and visualised in the image of a pubescent boy, clad in pyjamas, searching an exquisitely lit pile of potatoes for one that most resembled himself (see image, far right). The group poetry that gave rise to this image hints at the emotional confusion, frustrations and anxieties, as well as the physical changes, of the adolescent male:

> My soul is an empty warehouse, full of potential, stilled like a goldfish in a bowl.
> I am a small old shed inhabited by the biographies of the person

Left:
'Welcome', *Boychild*, 2007.
Right:
'Unfamiliar sproutings',
Boychild, 2007.
Andrew Whittuck

I am yet to be
How can you understand me if I do not understand myself?
I cannot draw myself complete. My body fills my mind.
Why do men's hearts give out before women's?
I dig my hands into the earth, fingers curl around unfamiliar forms.
As my body sprouts I am an oddly shaped potato.
(*Boychild* book, June 2007)

Learning about science

There is evidence that young children's informal learning about science in particular comes from everyday experience of where science connects with family or community. The final performance of *Boychild* followed a storyline with participants presenting narratives that could be understood in terms of scientific content. Such content was not explained; it was left to the audience to make the connections and to recognise the recurring themes of the development of the male, puberty, ageing, fatherhood and birth, the interplay between genetic inheritance and upbringing and the science of gender. At times factual information was given, but rarely; instead a series of images was presented, each rooted in the *Boychild* narrative, and either loosely or more directly connected to a scientific concept.

Rather than setting out to engage participants with particular science knowledge, *Boychild* started with a framework that invited groups to identify their own views, experiences and interests in response to a given set of stimuli. Such an approach enables young people to make decisions about the focus, content and nature of their involvement and can be highly motivating. But such methods are also often in conflict with the predetermined learning outcomes and performance measurement of science and other curricula, as is acknowledged by the Head of Drama in the secondary school:

> Most of all…[*Boychild*] was a reminder of how extraordinary and profound arts work can be when it is not bound by curriculum and other constraints and when the focus of the work comes from the individual. (Janice Wrigley, personal communication, 12 August 2007)

Site-specific performance and situated learning

Theories of 'situated learning', or learning embedded in social processes and physical contexts, can be applied to the extended and immersive experiences employed in *Visiting Time* and *Boychild*. Situated learning is active and engaged learning from doing, understanding gained through experience and participation in activities in relationships with others (Lave and Wenger, 1991). In *Visiting Time* the relationships and the learning were mediated through their placement in a working hospital. In *Boychild* the arts process depended on a meticulously constructed metaphorical space described by artist Mark Storor as a place "in which to explore masculinity differently, to negotiate and renegotiate the parameters of maleness". In literal terms this involved the creation of a new space at the Southwell Park site.

Following the threads of the narratives unearthed in the drama process took learners to a range of physical spaces both formal and informal, familiar and unfamiliar: school halls and classrooms, a science centre, a redundant MOD building, a prison education wing, a hospital maternity class, a bakery, a working man's club and even an undertaker's premises. As the material was gathered, different kinds of learning encounter were planned in response, so that students engaged in a wide range of different types of social interaction. Such learning also took place at times outside the usual rhythms and routines of school or institution, and with authentic, real-life goals and deadlines, not the often artificial goals of curriculum assessment.

When learning derives from social participation and shared experience, the spaces and places where learning takes place become powerful instruments. This is particularly true in institutions such as schools, hospitals or prisons where the uses of spaces are often potent symbolic reflections of lived experiences. The prison cell is an instrument of discipline, power and control. To experiment with such spaces, literally taping the dimensions of a cell onto the floor enabled us to suspend such power relationships and to revisit collectively the time spent by each young man alone within these parameters.

The young men from Portland Young Offenders Institution could not take part in an actual performance. Instead, they discussed how they wished to be embodied – as a male fetus before birth. An 18-year-old boy in a glass tank, lit carefully, speaks the thoughts of the unborn child; we, the audience are viewing a scan of a child yet to be born (see image, p. 124). This may reflect several associated ideas. 'Are we born criminal?', the young men had asked. Both womb and cell represent a fixed 'sentence', both a confinement of sorts. But there the similarity ends, for the womb represents a period of consistent and unconditional nurture. The prison cell, on the other hand, could be perceived as the consequence of later boyhood nurturing: "didn't you beat me when I could not spell 'red' R.E.A.D." (*Boychild* soundtrack, Jules Maxwell, June 2007). The womb is everybody's initial state of innocence, the prison cell reserved for those we exclude from society. The performance of the grown-boy fetus in his womb-like cell provided a view of 'Boychild' as full of potential, yet subject to labelling, misunderstandings, and a violent outside world:

I have no memory of you father...no memory I care to cherish
You burn your beats into my heart, into my skin
Like a toppled iron, sizzling on my arm
This is when men scream
Etched, I am branded
(*Boychild* soundtrack, Jules Maxwell, June 2007)

What kinds of learning took place?

In his bestselling work on emotional intelligence, Daniel Goleman
(1996) emphasises the importance in young children of emotional
intelligence, with its influence on personal qualities such as
empathy, self-awareness, negotiation and analysis of social
interactions. In arts learning and, arguably, particularly within a
drama process, the exploring of individual stories and the
rehearsing and revisiting of lived experiences offer powerful
opportunities for emotional learning, alongside the logical and
linguistic development involved in factual learning. This was
reflected in the words of a young participant in *Visiting Time*:

> [The presence in the group of a young patient] helped us to
> understand cystic fibrosis in a way which we wouldn't have
> understood if we had learned it just during lesson times. We
> actually felt what it must be like to live with a genetic disease and
> what people deal with every single minute of their lives. (Sir
> John Colfox School student, April 2004)

A primary school head teacher identified emotional learning as one
of the most valuable aspects of the work:

> For boys of 7–8 yrs old there's often not a huge awareness...and
> sensitivity towards others...and I feel that over the course of the
> year they developed both a self-awareness and a greater
> sensitivity to both the needs of others and the demands that
> others place upon them. (Bridport Primary School Head
> Teacher, July 2007)

Given what we know about emotional intelligence it is perhaps not surprising that the young boys (aged seven when we started) identified their turbulent emotional landscape as the starting-point for their drama process. The ensuing process offered them a means to explore and understand their emotions and behaviours, perhaps even in some cases to manage them better. It also offered them space to reflect on this learning and to understand something of its relevance beyond school. *Boychild* provided a framework that enabled young participants to engage with older males and to cross the boundaries of the places in which they are most used to learning. This challenged some underlying assumptions: that learning takes place in age-based groups, and that the primary context for learning is classroom-based tasks. An iterative cycle of reflection and review ensured that hearing and reflecting on the views of others was an important part of building a range of perspectives and understanding the foundations for other peoples' perceptions, attitudes and beliefs.

> Before I did *Boychild*, I did not listen much to other people. I thought what other people had to say wasn't important, but now I think it's very important. (Bridport Primary School student, July 2007)

The sincere comment of an eight-year-old who summed up his experience in the words "I learnt what it is like to be a man not a boy" (Bridport Primary School student, July 2007) reflects his appreciation that he had been given an opportunity to consider his ideas in relation to people and factors outside the usual relationships to be found within school. His Head Teacher also acknowledged the potential for learning outside the classroom:

> ...classrooms do restrict children's opportunities, and so when they are outside the classroom and especially when they're working with people who are asking quite challenging questions that's when children really feel that they are in a position to say

what they like… (Bridport Primary School Head Teacher, July 2007)

It is also a feature of situated learning that transferring learning between informal and formal settings is not a natural or straightforward process. While the majority of the students in *Boychild* were studying sciences, the tightly assessed nature of the A-level syllabus gave the students neither the conceptual space nor the time to connect directly the two forms of learning. Students themselves associate their learning primarily with drama and the arts, perceiving it to have little relevance to the science curriculum. Yet they go on to describe complex learning:

My learning was always happening, I learnt so much, such as what it's like to be male from the view of so many males of all ages from small to old.

I have gained a good insight into how the male body is different from a female, not only the obvious physical differences, but also the psychological and I have begun to grasp why our stereotype has become what it is, and what position men are expected to play in society. (Sir John Colfox School student, July 2007)

These reflections reveal that they are making connections between ways of knowing things and linking their activities with wider realms of social and personal understanding, as well as thinking deeply about concepts with a strong connection to science.

Pedagogical issues

These projects were intended to stimulate debate, to examine social, cultural and ethical issues, to encourage new ways of thinking, and to innovate. They did not set out to 'teach' scientific ideas or meet specific curricular objectives. They involved collaborative open-ended experiments in which scientific ideas and concepts were encountered and investigated in response to priorities identified by participants, supported where appropriate by scientists and scientific knowledge. Scientific ideas and concepts ran through the work in images, words, actions and sometimes meanings that went beyond words. The science learning that resulted is subtle, tacit learning, difficult to pin down, perhaps not yet discernible in some instances.

The learning in *Boychild* and *Visiting Time* came as much from the engagement and curiosity that gave rise to questions as from the answers that we sought from scientists or others. There are some questions to which science offers a number of responses, but not a complete answer:

How can I make a snowball when my hands are always hot?

Does my talent live in my genes or does it come with practice?

How many feelings does a boy have in a day, 50, 150, 1000, 25, 100, 1, 9999, 1 billion?

Why do men's hearts give out before women's?

Was I born to be a criminal?

In some cases factual knowledge can be sought – a visit to the science centre or an interview with a geneticist. Both serve to confirm that the deeper questions of science and their connection with lived experience do not have straightforward answers. What are important here are not the answers but the questions and the natural curiosity that emerges from the arts process, a prerequisite of successful science learning (Simon, 2001).

Science is everywhere and it matters most to us at the point when it intersects with our own lives. In many respects *Boychild* and *Visiting*

Time were hugely ambitious, blurring the boundaries between various practices: participatory arts, applied theatre and science education. They were experiments in providing an expanded space for learning presenting science enmeshed with human stories, acknowledging the emotions as well as the intellect and seeking to make it relevant to the lives of real people. In a deeply embodied learning process they created 'communities of curiosity' with the skills and motivations to take real responsibility, to apply knowledge beyond the classroom, to made connections between ways of knowing, and to reflect and review learning along the way.

> It allowed scientific learning to become immediate, sensory and deeply personal. It invited participants to find beauty in science, and to recognize the critical judgments involved in making art.
> (Helen Nicholson, Guardian Unlimited, 20 June 2007)

My thanks are due to all who participated in *Boychild* and *Visiting Time*, to Alex Coulter and above all to a unique artist and collaborator, Mark Storor.

Bibliography

Arends B, Thackara D (eds). Experiment: Conversations in art and science. London: The Wellcome Trust; 2003.

Bentley T. Learning Beyond the Classroom: Education for a changing world. London and New York: Demos; 1998.

Callanan A, Braswell G. Parent-child conversations about science and literacy. In Z Bekerman et al. (eds). Learning in Places: The informal education reader. New York: Peter Lang Publishing; 2006. pp. 123–39.

Goleman D. Emotional Intelligence: Why it can matter more than IQ. London: Bloomsbury; 1996.

Lave J, Wenger E. Situated Learning: Legitimate peripheral participation. New York: Cambridge University Press; 1991.

Nicholson H. Applied Drama: The gift of theatre. London: Macmillan; 2005.

Nicholson H. At last – educational theatre that can be called art. Guardian Unlimited 2007 20 June. http://blogs.guardian.co.uk/theatre/2007/06/sitespecific.html [accessed 4 January 2008].

Piaget J. The Language and Thought of the Child. New York: Meridian; 1974.

Simon H. "Seek and ye shall find": how curiosity engenders discovery. In K Crowley et al. (eds). Designing for Science: Implications from everyday, classroom, and professional settings. Mahwah, NJ: Erlbaum; 2001. pp. 5–20.

States B. The actor presence: three phenomenal modes. In P Zarrilli (ed.). Acting (Re) Considered: A theoretical and practical guide. London and New York: Routledge; 1995.

Stoetzler M, Yuval-Davis N. Standpoint theory, situated knowledge and the situated imagination. Feminist Theory 2002;3:315.

Thompson J. Applied theatre: bewilderment and beyond. In K Richards (ed.). Stage and Screen Studies, Vol. 5. Oxford: Peter Lang; 2006.

Introducing narrative

Ralph Levinson

The word 'narrative' derives from the Sanskrit 'gnarus' (knowing) and the Latin 'narro' (tell). In medieval times, storytelling combined with juggling and other forms of theatre were popular acrivities. The narrative story thus combines wisdom with street credibility and frivolity. Narrative conveys what is known, and can take various forms – drama, cartoon, film, dance. Allowing people to tell and listen, to talk of experiences not understood or imagined by others, narrative is an organiser for these experiences by structuring and sequencing events.

Since science is made and done by humans it does yield narratives as lived experience. Until quite recently the prevalent stories published in school science textbooks were heroic, celebrating the lives and breakthroughs of individual scientists, such as Pasteur and Jenner, and the impact of their discoveries on the welfare of humankind. But paralleling these grand narratives have been localised and personal narratives around contemporary science, for example, people affected by pollutants as waste from local industries or parents-to-be, who as carriers of a genetic condition, are seeking advice about what action to take.

How such personal, and often collective, narratives can link to personal stories and acts of political organisation, resistance and social solidarity can be exemplified in the story of the neem tree. This ancient tree has been celebrated and used for many years for its fungicidal, medicinal and contraceptive properties, and is popularly known as the 'village pharmacy' of South Asia. Neem trees were planted in avenues when New Delhi was built because of the coolness of their shade. In 1995 a patent was granted to a US multinational company on an antifungal product that could be extracted from the neem. This meant that the neem was no longer a resource for the rural population of India but the property of an American corporation. Led by the environmentalist and physicist Vandana Shiva, local people mobilised to successfully resist the patent, which they perceived as bio-piracy. Political organisation and publicity formed around the stories that villagers could recount about the cultural and scientific importance of the neem tree to their ways of life over thousands of years.

This power of narrative to "see the lives of the different" (Nussbaum, 1997, p. 88) and make the invisible visible underpins Angela Calabrese Barton and Tara O'Neill's article about a group of New York inner-city schoolchildren, the 'Fabulous Five', who decide to make a video about their lives and about what science means to them. There are similarities in the politics and structure of the stories they come to tell to that of the neem tree because the Fabulous Five are re-appropriating science as part of the story of their lives. For them, science as taught in school is decontextualised and distant, but their understanding is transformed as science comes to have meaning for issues which concern them. Their stories are characterised as counter-storytelling both in challenging the dominant school narratives of science from which the Fabulous Five feel marginalised and in providing a sense of community where they seek to use science to participate in society. Barton and O'Neill identify the underlying themes of counter-storytelling: 'valuing place', which incorporates social, political, cultural and historical dimensions, mediates the relationship between the children and science. 'Hybridity' is revealed in the cultural resources such as dance and music that the children draw on to tell the story of science that illuminates their experiences. There are overtones of hybridity in a story Vandana Shiva tells about the festival of *Akti* in central India, where families from the villages perform a ritual bringing their rice in folded leaves; the rice is mixed and exchanged, demonstrating the dangers of isolated, pure-bred rice being vulnerable to disease. And in 're-constructing authority' the Fabulous Five have shifted the locus of power away from their teachers to a point where they become active participants in telling the story of science.

Reclaiming science by those marginalised by education is also the theme of Catherine McNamara and Alison Rooke's article on Sci:dentities. In this project, young transsexual and transgendered people generated their personal narratives in the forms of interviews, weblogs and 'zines through a process of subverting common-sense biological assumptions about sex and gender. The detailed and informed discussion with medical professionals highlights problems of understanding and the limitations of extant scientific resources in supporting the young trans people's self-understanding. The insights shown by these young people and the transformative experiences of telling their stories in creating new works of art have many commonalities with the Fabulous Five. They have to find a new way of drawing on a science that they find self-affirming and consistent with their lived realities. In the process they are reconstructing authority and, as with the Fabulous Five, it is the collective experience which is crucial in supporting their developing personal narratives. What has science come to mean for them? As one of the participants says: "science is...always changing and adapting to personal experiences and social movements. And if it isn't, it should be!"

These articles demonstrate an awareness of the constraints as well as the possibilities of the science curriculum, that science can make links with personal narratives that are very powerful and a social role for change, but it is not a straightforward process. The forms of narratives can present distinct challenges. Kerry Chappell's article on embodied narratives asks questions about the ways in which dance can narrate scientific and socio-scientific ideas. Chappell draws on the idea of a spectrum of intimacy in describing the relationships between dance artists and scientists. At one end there are the kinds of connection that science teachers are familiar with, exploiting movement to reinforce a chemical change or to demonstrate 'invisible' concepts such as the motion and arrangement of atoms in space. But at the other end of the spectrum, the nature of the relationship between dance and science is complex and distinct from other forms of narrative such as written stories or videos. Chappell draws on a range of examples and collaborations between scientists and artists – genetics and neurophysiology – to unravel the mechanism of embodied narratives. To engage and understand in these collaborations is a difficult but rewarding process.

Caution is needed in relocating these ideas in the science classroom. The articles on counter-storytelling and Sci:dentities tell of narratives that emerged from a sense of social dissatisfaction. The process of developing fruitful narratives, as also shown in Chappell's article, demands commitment, knowledge and organisation from everyone involved. But the approaches used show that an ability to draw on the resource of narrative can open windows on what it is to do and understand science, and the creative relationship of science to self-knowledge and social change.

Bibliography
Nussbaum M. Cultivating humanity. Cambridge, MA: Harvard University Press; 1997.

Counter-storytelling in science: authoring a place in the worlds of science and community

Angela Calabrese Barton
Tara O'Neill

Angela Calabrese Barton and *Tara O'Neill* document how young people from a deprived inner-city school construct their own stories of science by making a video, transforming substantive school science into a medium that promotes active dialogue between them and their schoolfriends. Three themes emerge from this analysis: the importance of place, cross-cultural fusion or 'hybridity', and renegotiation of authority. This analysis shows that in making science come alive for the participants the students created novel contexts for science and citizenship.

In this chapter we explore the experiences of five middle-school young people from a low-income community and their 20-minute video about 'life and science' in the inner city they produced as part of a voluntary after-school programme. We view the video project as an example of the students' efforts to tell their 'counter-stories' of middle-school science. We develop three themes around counter-storytelling in science: sense of place, hybridity and reconstructing authority. We use these findings to challenge standard notions of achievement in science, which is especially relevant given that the young people in this chapter attend a 'failing school'. We conclude with a discussion of the ways in which this video project might advance our understandings of the relationship between teaching and learning science, and citizenship.

Introduction

In the closing four minutes and 15 seconds of *What We Bring to Science*,[1] a 20-minute video about what five sixth-grade (11 and 12 years old) students know about science and want others to understand, the song 'The World's Greatest', sung by R Kelly, plays prominently in the background. Timed with the lyrics, 37 scenes fade in and out, each one blended into the next, and each lasting between four and eight seconds. The scenes, some of which are still photos, some of which are video, move rhythmically between images of the neighbourhood, the school, the science classroom and the schoolyard. In each of the images the young people are always positioned in-action, talking and/or doing science in ways that deeply reflect their lives inside and outside of school.

The combination of images and song express the emotion of these young people that they are more than children who live in a dangerous neighbourhood and attend a failing school. They are the hope of their neighbourhood and the school. They are students who strive to blend their sense of place with their science knowledge in order to better everyone's understanding of themselves and their neighbourhood. In this final scene we are immediately struck by the juxtaposition of young people enacting a sense of place and importance in the worlds of school and science, and images of a school and neighbourhood known throughout the city as a place of despair – of students failing school, of schools failing communities, of too many lives ended too soon.

Yet a frame-by-frame analysis of the final scene reveals stubborn young people, physically and artistically positioning themselves as powerful, dominant and positive members of their neighbourhood and their school community. These scenes, serving as a final storyline, recap the earlier episodes presented in the video. In nearly all of the scenes, young people loom in the foreground of their pictures, with blurred activity happening behind them. Ten scenes show young people doing science in out-of-school settings in ways that combine their activity and knowledge of how the world works, such as the scenes where young people are running, dancing, planting flowers or playing basketball (see figure 1).

Above, from top to bottom:
Figure 1: planting flowers behind the school.

Figure 2: holding up science poster from school science.

Figure 3: debating 'who knows science' in the district science lab classroom.

A Calabrese Barton and T O'Neill

Six scenes highlight young people's accomplishments in school science through the presentation of student work and showing images of students participating in school science classes and after-school programmes (see figure 2). Six more scenes show images of young people debating scientific ideas in a variety of contexts (see figure 3).

As the montage's still photos and video clips fade in and out in time to the music, one gets the sense that the young people are seeking to position themselves with epistemic authority, on equal footing with their teachers and other school leaders. As the scenes flash from school to neighbourhood, one also gets the sense that the young people who made this movie make claim to their city and their place within it. For example, nine scenes show neighbourhood hotspots, young people hanging out, or issues of concern such as the trash piles or a street known for gang fights. The despair that often dominates the talk about this and similar neighbourhoods in popular media and research is conspicuously absent from this closing scene, replaced by a message of what these young people indeed do bring to science – intellectually, materially and culturally.

We begin with this overview of the final scene of *What We Bring to Science* because in our work with urban young people growing up in economically impoverished communities we witness time and time again the myriad of creative and artistic ways they seek to author spaces for participation in science and in their worlds (Calabrese Barton, 1998; Rahm, 2002). If one were to view the video production *What We Bring to Science* with only the knowledge that it was generated by sixth-grade students in a voluntary programme, we predict that not many would guess the video was produced by a group of young people who attend school in the poorest community in New York City with the lowest city test scores. The combination of who the young people are, where they come from and the story they want to tell is what brings power to their message.

School science typically emphasises the importance of developing conceptual understandings of scientific phenomena, with little attention given to how or why students might use scientific ideas or thinking in their engagement with life outside of schools. In the remainder of this chapter we unpack the video production, *What We Bring to Science*, in order to demonstrate the problem of just *how* it is we come to know young people and how this frames what we expect of them as science learners and members of a larger global society. Their constructions in the video project are an example of their efforts to create spaces for 'counter-stories' of middle-school science. We develop three themes around counter-storytelling in science: sense of place, hybridity and reconstructing authority. Our discussion of the young people's role in the video will challenge standard notions of achievement in science, which is especially relevant given that the young people in this chapter attend a 'failing school'. We conclude with a discussion of the ways in which this video project might advance our understandings of the relationship between science and citizenship.

Counter-storytelling and urban young people

The discourse surrounding urban science education in the USA has tended to focus on the problems or challenges faced primarily by young people from low-income and African-American and Latina/o backgrounds. By and large, students from these demographic groups are lagging behind their peers in school success as evidenced by high-stakes achievement scores, grades and admission to selective high schools and colleges. At the same time, they often attend schools that are vastly under-resourced in terms of curricular materials, laboratory equipment, course offerings, and experienced and qualified teachers. While this discourse captures a dimension of life in urban schooling that is real and problematic, it offers a very narrow depiction of what it means to be urban, African-American, Latina/o, or low-income. It "essentializes and wipes out the complexities and richness of a group's cultural life" (Montecinos, 1995, p. 293) and limits the education community's abilities to respond to the needs and development of such young people.

Scholars from critical race theory have argued that it is important to move outside of discourses of problem, failure and deficit to understand and act upon the experiences of marginalised individuals (Delgado and Stefanic, 2001). They argue that we need to find ways to understand how issues of race and ethnicity intersect with class and gender to frame not only the experiences individuals have but also how those experiences are understood and taken up by others – for example, the need to uncover how institutional stories, like those about school failure and achievement, the authority of science, and who can participate in science, are not neutral or objective. Further, these scholars argue about the need of marginalised students to tell of new ways of understanding the challenges and possibilities of urban education. It is from this standpoint that we believe counter-storytelling to be vitally important.

Counter-storytelling has been defined by Delgado (1995) as the telling of stories of and by people whose experiences are not often told, such as low-income African-American and Latina/o young people in urban schools. Counter-storytelling can serve as a tool for exposing, analysing and challenging the stories of those in power, which are often a part of dominant discourse. Counter-storytelling can build community among those at the margins, challenge the perceived wisdom of those at society's centre by providing a context to transform established belief systems, and show new and different possibilities by combining elements of the story and the current reality.

Urban young people engage in counter-storytelling all of the time, whether or not the story is recognised by those in schools or by dominant society at large. Indeed, storytelling has a rich and continuing tradition in African-American and Latina/o communities. We believe that counter-storytelling is an especially important way to understand how urban young people choose to engage with science and how they seek to use science to establish their participation in society. While the counter-stories of urban young people take many forms – from their everyday recounting of personal experience in the classroom to the co-construction of narratives in after-school banter – we have become particularly interested in how a group of five young people constructed a more formal counter-story about science and their lives through digital storytelling.

Urban young people telling counter-stories
The Fabulous Five

What We Bring to Science was made by a group of five sixth-grade students (Star, Melanie, Jose, Jasmine and Adel)[2] as part of a voluntary after-school and lunchtime science–technology club. The students named their production group Fabulous Five because there were five of them and they thought they were "fabulous". The Fabulous Five investigated, wrote and produced the movie with the support of their club teacher (Tara O'Neill), with the goal of presenting a completed movie to the entire sixth-grade community – about 180 students. The theme of the movie focused on what they felt they brought to science and how they would use it to teach others science. As Adel explains (see figure 4):

Above:
Figure 4: Adel explaining the purpose of the movie.
A Calabrese Barton and T O'Neill

> The main focus of this video is to make people that do not know, people that know very little, very little about science, for them to understand. Instead of giving them the science textbook, which would take years for them to finally understand it, we are taking the textbook, breaking it down into pieces for them and then when they see our video they will understand it easier.

The students in the Fabulous Five attended a large streamed or setted 'failing' neighbourhood middle school that serves a predominantly low-income and African-American and Hispanic population. The members of the Fabulous Five reflected the ethnic, social and economic make-up of the school: two of the students were Puerto Rican, one was Dominican, one was first-generation American with both parents from Ghana, and one was African-American. All of the students qualified for free school meals. The school structured its classes around a tracking system consisting of honours, moderate and lower-level classes. One of the students was in the honors class while the other four were in the lower-level class.

To understand the intentions of the Fabulous Five as they set out to tell their science counter-story it is important to understand how the video project and the Fabulous Five came into existence. The Fabulous Five was initially started when one of the students, Star, asked Tara if he could help her edit some video footage Tara had taken during a science and literacy project that she, Angie[3] and the teachers had conducted at their school. Tara agreed and suggested that Star invite a group of friends. The group expanded beyond Star's friends as two other students who had heard about the project joined in. At the third meeting of the club the students collectively informed Tara they wanted to make "[their] own movie about science," implying that the video footage of their classroom lives did not capture what they wanted others to 'learn' about them. They had told us that they did not find the video of their classrooms very interesting and that they wanted to use the cameras to film things about science they cared about. They were clear that they were less interested in watching their teachers talk than in having the opportunity to capture themselves and their peers on film talking and doing science. While the narrative of *What We Bring to Science* unfolded over time as students moved through the various phases of production, the conversation at this third meeting brought to the surface the young people's desires to use film to 'give voice in science' to themselves and their peers.

Tara and Angie agreed, and the group settled upon making a movie about how they viewed and used science in their everyday lives. The group first generated a storyboard for their movie, deciding upon both the content storyline and how to generate the information needed for the movie. They decided that they would: (a) interview their classmates to determine what they cared about with respect to science, and that they would use these ideas as the key themes of their movie; (b) collect much of their video footage

outside of their school in order to explain how their lives mattered in science; and (c) not have adults, such as teachers or parents, appear as the science experts. They wanted the movie to be about what they brought to science, and believed that they were the experts on this topic.

The Fabulous Five's counter-storytelling

The video opens with ominous music playing in the background and a clap of thunder as "presented by... The Fabulous Five" runs across the screen in red text set against a black background. The video then shifts immediately in tone and feel by presenting a view of the front of the school, with Adel standing in front. Star narrates: "This is our school. This is where we do all our work. And whoever is seeing this video, I hope they like it. This is our territory," (see figure 5). As the camera pans away from the school and into the neighbourhood a steady urban music beat fades in. The next minute and a half provide moving images of the neighbourhood as the young people move around the sidewalk perimeter of their school, filming as they go. Cars and buses ride by the front of the school. Elevated subway trains move back and forth, with their rumble overpowering the young people's talk. The camera glides by trash piles on the sidewalks, and presents an image of a five-storey school building taken from behind the metal fence that bounds and separates the school from its neighbourhood (see figure 6). The tour is highlighted by a close-up of a street locally referred to as 'Broken Hill' because of the almost gravel-like consistency of the pavement and a guided walk down another local street on the opposite end of the school block called 'Snake Hill' (see figure 7). The students explain that "we named it Snake Hill" because it winds around like a snake. Melanie explains that her father says Snake Hill "reminds him of the Dominican Republic where he grew up".

Above, from top to bottom:
Figure 5: Star in the opening scene.

Figure 6: Fabulous Five's school.

Figure 7: Snake Hill.

Figure 8: skin debate.

A Calabrese Barton and T O'Neill

The images are then disrupted by the title frame, which, like the beginning frame, presents red text with a black backdrop. Six-and-a-half minutes are then taken up by a series of scenes that involve young people talking about science. The major thrust of the talk is about 'knowing science'. While Adel leads most of these short scenes by playing the role of reporter and asking her peers what they think about science, some of these scenes involve young people debating ideas that they want others to know something about. For example, in one scene, Adel, Melanie and Jose are in the school science laboratory discussing with each other why they all have a slightly different skin colour from each other (see figure 8). Jose argues that skin colour is due to the sun, but is interrupted by Melanie explaining that "skin has melanin and darker skin has more melanin than lighter skin". Adel then turns to the camera and offers an explanation that is a compromise of sorts. She explains:

> You turn darker by a sun tan. [Pointing to Jose, a lighter-skinned student] He has less melanin, so he has the ability, if he goes out into the sun, he will turn darker faster than me. He will turn darker quicker than I will turn darker. It will take him approximately to my calculations five minutes and me ten minutes [to turn the same amount of darkness]. (8'07–8'27)

These formal scenes of young people talking science are divided by short, poignant clips, which call into question exactly how science is being defined or taken up in the video. Clearly, in the scene above, how young people think about and present the challenge of talking science centres on their lived experiences in a racialised world. Whether it actually takes Adel an extra five minutes in the sun to become as dark as Jose is not really as central as how the young people raise the problem of understanding and explaining skin pigmentation.

In another scene, a student is standing in the science lab describing how everyone knows science: "I think everyone knows science. You do science every day. If you recycle, that's science." The image cuts quickly to a cat walking under a car carrying a dead rat in its mouth and Star reporting: "That's how life is. People eat people. Animals eat animals." Again, we see the urban experiences of the young people framing how they 'know science'. The Fabulous Five were excited to include the cat scene because they believed it reflected how life is in the inner city. At the same time it conjured up an example of a standard middle-school science topic – the food chain. Another example involves a clip of a young boy asking the question: "Are y'all doing that science thing?" This clip is repeated six times during the video, and is repeatedly used to challenge the viewer to consider 'what is that science thing?'

While many of the scenes show young people talking about science in the classroom setting, the focus of their talk is often more personal than a classroom setting conveys. For example, Adel interviews a fellow sixth-grader, Rita, who states that "science to me is very important because you learn what you got inside of you. And what nutrients you need. The reason why I mostly like science is that I want to be a doctor when I grow up." This interview and two others similar to it are sandwiched with close-up views of a student's eyes and mouth, a boy dancing, and the "Are y'all doing that science thing?" clip. Many of the examples used by the students to talk about science in their lives also connect deeply to the kinds of activities that young people are typically engaged in but are not often talked about as science, like dance or cats eating rats. As Adel says, "I wasn't going to consider dancing part of science, but then when you just said it, I was like oh yeah dancing, when you move you use up energy and sweat, so that is a form of science."

The next four-and-a-half minutes shifts focus from talking about and doing science in school to the neighbourhood and the young people's roles and lives in that setting. The mood shifts as the song 'That's Just the Way it is' (by Bruce Hornsby) comes into the background. Star opens the transition by stating: "This is our neighbourhood. There is not much to know other than it is dangerous. I be here most of the time." Vivid images and stories of

Above, from top to bottom:
Figure 9: backside view of the school.

Figure 10: graffiti in school yard.

Figure 11: Jason dancing.

*A Calabrese Barton
and T O'Neill*

the neighbourhood are presented. The school is again viewed through the metal bars that separate it from the neighbourhood (see figure 9). The young people pan in on a detailed graffiti illustration at the back end of the schoolyard and different streets running to and from the schoolyard (figure 10). At one point, the students co-narrate a description of Snake Hill, a residential neighbourhood setting directly behind the school:

Star: We walking through Snake Hill. We named it as
           Snake Hill. Not us –
Melanie: My father says it reminds him of
           [the Dominican Republic] because it turns,
           its like it goes from there.
Star: It's not just us in particular. It's not just us
           in particular.

As the students lead the viewer to the bottom of Snake Hill the viewer is taken just outside of the far end of the schoolyard and across the street from the beginning of Davidson Avenue, where the young people explain:

Star: See this is the most dangerous street of all. There be
           shootouts over here. I wouldn't like to be here.
Melanie: It be crazy. That's why I go up this way. You saw my
           mother [walking up the hill and around to avoid this
           street], we don't walk here. I would not like to be here.
           That's why I go this way [pointing back up Snake Hill].
Star: Davidson, there be shootouts and everything.
Melanie: Yea, slicin' people. It be crazy.
Star: I don't want to be on this street.

Ironically (or perhaps not so ironically), as the students narrate this story in real time, a police siren can be heard blazing, adding both a sense of urgency and depth to their story. Yet the scene easily fades into the next, showing a group of girls, then two of the Fabulous Five dancing with verve and youthful optimism (figure 11):

Melanie: Go ahead keep on dancin'.

Adel and Star dance their way towards the camera. As they approach, Melanie begins to direct their dancing.

Melanie: Star, shake.

As Star is shaking to the beat, he takes off his hat to put it on in dance step. However, his hat comes over his eyes and he states:

Star: That was not supposed to happen.
Melanie: But it did.

While the tone of this second section is heavy at times, the young people reflect resilience to their situation, reminding the viewer that "that's just the way it is" and despite the challenges they "keep on dancin'". This last scene bleeds into the final scene discussed at the beginning of the chapter.

Making sense of the Fabulous Five's counter-story: valuing place, hybridity and authority

There are many things we, as teachers and researchers, have learned about what the Fabulous Five bring to science, including a deep interest in understanding how their bodies work, a desire to make science accessible to younger people, and a strong sense of pride in identifying themselves as people who know and do science. Cutting across these themes are vibrant messages of the role of place in science learning, the importance of hybridity and reconstructions of authority.

Valuing place

A sense of place, or a living ecological dialectic relationship between a person and a place, plays a vital role in how individuals and communities make meaning in the world (Gruenwald, 2003). Yet, in an age in US education politics when an 'anywhere and anytime' approach to establishing national standards and assessments dominates, seeing place in students' constructions of their worlds is often given short shrift. Place, however, foregrounds what the Fabulous Five bring to science. The theme of what the young people know about science is driven by their place-based experiences of playing basketball, dancing, graffiti art, skin colour and test-driven school practices. Their talk about the science in these experiences is drawn from several sources, blending more subjective talk of their feelings and experiences with more objective, science-like talk. For example, in the movie (3'55–8'31), the Fabulous Five first interview students to find out what they think science is. Interviews with several students reveal a common theme to be understanding our bodies: "When it comes to science I am learning about myself. I am learning about what I got inside of me," (Star, 5'56–6'03). Interspersing these interviews are short scenes where members of the Fabulous Five can be seen discussing or debating with their peers ideas about how the body works, such as why we sweat, and why different colours of skin tan at different rates. Peppered throughout their talk are references to family experiences, textbook ideas, knowledge gained from reading product labels, and personal feelings and opinions, such as when Melanie describes her experiences on the playground and at the store: "Let's say if you want to buy Clorox. So then, it says [on the bottle] how the Clorox was made. What's the ingredients. What it does. What does it do if you have it on your hand."

'Place' is a complex term, involving not just the physical location in which something takes place, but also the social, cultural, political and historical dimensions. Young people's talk about and knowledge of science throughout the movie is operationalised along many dimensions of place, including history, geography, culture, and biology. For example, in the scene where they capture the close-up image of the cat walking under the car with a rat in its mouth (see figure 12), the students seamlessly move between talk about the food chain and cultural politics: "That's how life is.

People eat people. Animals eat animals," (Star, 3'41–3'49). In the two scenes prior to the cat scene, there is a clip where three students are discussing how Native Americans' knowledge of how plants grow is related to science (figure 13). As explained by two of the three students being interviewed:

Student 1: You know how, like a lot time ago, like the Native Americans, they live in the wilderness and they would get everything they need from the wilderness.
Student 2: Oh, yeah they know science!
Student 1: Yeah, they have to know science because that's basically the way they lived.
Student 2: They won't survive, they survived by growing stuff so...
Student 1: Yeah, so they have like a knowledge of science.

Thus it is not just 'who' knows science that is framed interdimensionally, but also 'what' it means to know science.

Above, from top to bottom:
Figure 12: cat under car.

Figure 13: students discussing how Native Americans know science.

A Calabrese Barton and T O'Neill

Hybridity

Young people draw upon their sense of place to produce new, heterogeneous, hybrid knowledge and identities that characterise their engagement with science. *What We Bring to Science* offers a glimpse into how young people take up knowledge, resources and identities in novel ways that often go unsanctioned by school science. For example, the perspectives of members of the Fabulous Five and their viewers are those of particular kinds of learners in science with an access to science not always explicitly granted in science class. Melanie explained a third of the way into the movie:

We are making this so we could be able to teach younger students what we have learned with our teachers and about like let's say somebody in our class. I think it was Natalie or Raquel asked how come when you go in the water your fingers get wrinkly. Well, we don't have an answer for that yet but we'll find out. Just like the eighth-graders get science and they probably know about that. So they could probably make a video so they could show it to younger students like we're doing. So we could show it to the fifth-graders, fourth-graders, and the third-graders. (8'32–9'06)

We see hybridity in the choices the Fabulous Five make in their video presentation. The blending of music selections with scientific talk, of dancing and hanging out with school work, of neighbour-hood scenes with school scenes, and of social status with epistemic status reveals just how dynamic their efforts to foster hybridity are. A good example is the final scene referenced at the beginning of this chapter. In three minutes, 37 scenes are shown where young people are positioned in-action, talking about or doing science that is culturally relevant. Of the 37 scenes, over half take place outside of school with young people blending talk of neighbourhoods with talk of science. As explained by members of the Fabulous Five to their audience at a pre-conference session of the 2003 annual meeting of the National Association for Research in Science Teaching:

Adel: At the beginning of the movie we figured that all we're going to do is listen to Mr M, our science teacher last year, listen to him for a change so we could put it in the movie, and we could put it in the movie in a fun way. Then when we saw that, um, the things that we're learning…was outside [in the neighbourhood].

Audience: How did you decide what to put in the movie?

Star: We decided to put in the movie whatever concerned science like whatever we were trying to say. We decided that everything we showed we were going to write it on the bottom of the screen like say the ball was bouncing we going to say that's this is gravity and running it's like energy. We didn't have a chance

	to do that so we just explained it in less words.
Jose:	We showed them [younger students] what life science is. We talked about the melanin. We showed the cat eating the rat, and all that.

Thus, in the video we can see how young people orient themselves in ways different from what is usual in their school setting. The young people used science content from their school science classes and experiential knowledge from their neighbourhood to create a new means of participating in and a new conceptual understanding of science. In creating these hybrid moments, the Fabulous Five were able to claim authority in a context (school science) where such power had often been denied.

Reconstructing authority

The students used the video project as a way of participating and expressing epistemic authority in science. The Fabulous Five used two tools to gain epistemic authority. First, the students centred their discussions of science content in the movie on information that had been taught in their sixth-grade science class. They then purposefully shifted the focus of this content away from school science by basing the explanation of the content in the real-life context of their lives and the community. They also used interviews with students and student explanations of science concepts to make the point that this is not just a movie about young people, but about science. Like the melanin example described earlier, students weigh in as experts on how "sweat helps a runner" and why it is that Native Americans knew science because they grew food and needed to use science to survive.

Secondly, the students' narrative was marked by the absence of teachers or other adult voices. Many of the students in the video project described feeling that they were not an important part of their science class because their ideas were always less important than those presented by their teachers or their science texts. In the

Students had both time and
space to voice their ideas
and experiences in ways that
aligned with the practice of
school science as well as
challenging the traditional
practice of school science.

video project, the students had both time and space to voice their ideas and experiences in ways that aligned with the practice of school science as well as challenging the traditional practice of school science. For example, students often dutifully worked on tasks assigned by us such as the preparation of the storyboards or in selecting and researching topics that are traditional school science topics (such as the role of melanin in skin colour). Yet students also transformed these activities in order to make their experiences a part of them (for instance, when they use their understanding of melanin and skin colour to make numerical estimates of how long it would take for a person of a particular skin type to tan).

By being able to express their ideas, the students were able to demonstrate science capabilities that they felt were not valued in their school science classes and explain to others what they (as opposed to their teachers or a textbook) felt science was:

Tara:	So, looking back on it are you glad you did it? If so, why?
Star:	Yeah, because it was fun. It was a different experience than a regular project.
Tara:	Why was it a different experience than a regular project?
Star:	Because we had science and the real world out there and we had to put it together. We looked at everything and then we had to relate it to science.
Tara:	So, what was different about that?
Star:	You never see a teacher do a project like that. They don't assign projects like that.

In the end, what is made purposefully clear in the video as well as by Star in the quote above is that the Fabulous Five did not want to be excluded from science. To the contrary, this sense of exclusion in school science seemed to power their drive to produce a movie about the parts of themselves and science that they felt school science had missed. The Fabulous Five seized the opportunity of the video project to show others (their teachers, their peers and the greater community) that they could participate in science in ways that went above and beyond what had been expected of them. Instead of being excluded from science, the Fabulous Five used the video project to actively create their own narrative in science. By focusing all of their examples of science around topics and activities they had done (or could do) themselves, the Fabulous Five indicated that science was not just something done by other people in other places.

Conclusions

Producing *What We Bring to Science* generated the voice of young people in science, to explore what they cared about and to 'prove' their value in science and in their school community. As Star explains:

Star: Our whole argument was all about that we wanted to be professionals. We wanted to be professionals. We wanted to make a movie where people would be like, wow.

Tara: But, why did it matter that it was perfect?

Star: From my point of view, I guess we wanted to show what we were made of. To show other people that even though we were young or despite whatever grade we were in, that we were still smart and we were capable of doing whatever they did. If they did it we could do it too. We're not less than them.

Engaging counter-storytelling in science education we believe helps not only to dismantle stereotypes of who low-income urban young people are and what they bring to science, but also to challenge and expand the role of science education in fostering citizenship. It has often been written in the USA that students need to acquire a knowledge base and set of skills in order to participate in society as thoughtful, contributing members. Yet the Fabulous Five's counter-story reveals that the relationship between science and citizenship is much more complex, and involves the ongoing interactions young people have in society.

We acknowledge and place value on the ways in which young people's engagement in science in everyday life is intertwined with economics, politics, power and values, and has to do with their immediate rather than future lives. While the young people were not engaged in a community-wide problem, such as their community's enduring struggles with air quality and quality healthcare, they were immersed in their own equally valuable problem: how to raise the question of who can do science and what that looks like.

The Fabulous Five's production of *What We Bring to Science* is a story that counters the popular media picture of urban young people as disengaged, inexperienced and unaccomplished science students. Members of the group expressed frustration with school science because they felt that it was fundamentally about the ideas of the teacher and the science text. That they attended a school on the state's failing list and were submitted to page-a-day curriculum reform that often took the form of test preparation and basic skills development demonstrates that they placed as central their desire to educate others in ways that involve the learner. According to the Fabulous Five (FF), during a pre-session presentation at the 2003 annual meeting of the National Association for Research in Science Teaching, their mission was successful.

Jose: To me the whole movie was worth it because I left the school knowing that I got to show little kids what science really is in a better way than just in the classroom teaching them.

Audience: So would you say that teaching this way of you guys doing projects is better than the normal classroom way?

FF: Yeah!

Audience: Have you shown this to the teachers at your school?

FF: Yes.

Audience: Did it change any of their ways of teaching?

Star: Yeah.

Jasmine: Some of them.

Audience: Some of them. You're not going to get everybody right?

Star: Mostly science teachers.

Audience: So you got a few of them to change their style?

Star: Yeah, like Ms A. Sometimes she don't teach with textbooks no more.

Jose: We used to read out of a boring textbook, that's all we used to do.

Tara: Do you think that's a direct relation to seeing this movie?

Adel: Yeah, like Mr M. Last year he would just get on the projector and write like three pages of notes and put it and he'd say copy them, and he'd go sit down and when we leave class we're like uh what just happened and nobody will go back into their notes to read all that. So after he saw the movie it changed his way of teaching a lot.

Research for this paper was supported by the National Science Foundation (REC 0096032) and is acknowledged with gratitude. The opinions expressed in the paper are those of the authors and not those of the National Science Foundation.

1 See http://getcity.org/counterstory.html to watch the video.

2 All names used in the text are pseudonyms.

3 One of the authors.

Bibliography

Calabrese Barton A. Teaching Science for Social Justice. New York: Teachers College Press; 1998.

Delgado R. Critical Race Theory: The cutting edge. Philadelphia, PA: Temple University Press; 1995.

Delgado R, Stefanic J. Critical Race Theory: An introduction. New York: New York University Press; 2001.

Gruenewald DA. Foundations of place: a multidisciplinary framework for place-conscious education. American Educational Research Journal 2003;40(3):619–36.

Montecinos C. Culture as an ongoing dialogue: implications for multicultural teacher education. In C Sleeter, P McLaren (eds). Multicultural Education, Critical Pedagogy, and the Politics of Difference. Albany: State University of New York Press; 1995. pp. 269–308.

Rahm J. Emergent learning opportunities in an inner-city youth gardening program. Journal of Research in Science Teaching 2002;39(2):164–84.

Roth W-M, Désautels J. Educating for citizenship: reappraising the role of science education. Canadian Journal for Science, Mathematics, and Technology Education 2004;4:149–68.

Solorzano D, Yasso T. Critical race methodology: counter-storytelling as an analytical framework for education research. Qualitative Inquiry 2002;8,:23–44.

Embodied narratives

Kerry Chappell

Of all the art forms, dance might seem to offer the least opportunity for productive partnerships with science. Yet several groundbreaking collaborations have seen scientific concepts as complex as epigenetics and neural activity in the brain explored through dance. As *Kerry Chappell* points out, dance is fundamentally about creating an 'embodied narrative' in which the dynamics of the physical human form communicate meaning to an audience. Partnerships between dance artist and scientist can deconstruct scientific concepts and inspire performances that are both artistically successful and can communicate an essence of their scientific inspiration that words alone cannot convey.

Introduction

The idea of a creative collaboration between a scientist and a dance artist may initially seem a strange enterprise, bringing together two very different worlds that do not appear to have much in common. But these kinds of collaboration are increasing in both professional and educational settings in the UK, and for very good reasons. Recent collaborations have included, among others, a 'Choreographing for the Brain' project, a dance theatre work exploring the scientific explanations of left-handedness, and a touring dance-in-education piece investigating the science and issues of epigenetics.

As more of this kind of work is undertaken in schools, and more practitioners become skilled in developing collaborations, questions are being raised about the activity at the heart of this practice.[1] This chapter seeks to delve into these questions. It particularly focuses on how dance can create embodied narratives and meaning-making around socioscientific issues, and how developing understanding of these contributes to new interpretations of ideas and to new approaches.

Whether we experience dance as a performer or as an audience member, there is something special about the encounter that cannot be easily translated into words. It is difficult to explain any shift that may have occurred, but it stems from gleaning understanding via lived bodies rather than text or spoken words. It makes us rely on our 'embodiment', something non-dancers are perhaps not used to engaging with and interpreting, particularly within a science context.

Embodiment might be thought of in interacting layers: there is the ability to sense a movement or moving from within, there is also the ability to 'think physically', and then a capacity to move with an awareness of the whole physical self (Chappell, 2006). The American dance scholar and practitioner Sue Stinson pulls together these layers and how they interact to make a greater sum than their parts: "a way of perceiving oneself from the inside out, where one is aware of feeling, movements and intentions, rather than looking objectively from the outside in" (Stinson, 2004, p. 2). She argues that it is this ability to sense our embodiment that allows us to perceive and feel a dance and then understand our own response to it. For me, empathy – feeling an idea in someone else's shoes – is also a particularly important part of this process.

When experiencing and making meaning through this embodiment in dance, it is important not to be limited by an understanding of narrative as linear storytelling. This is certainly possible: a story might be told in dance from which an audience can take away a clear sequence of events. A dance may also be plotless, a work with abstract ideas (Preston-Dunlop, 1998). There is also the possibility that a narrative may exist in dance that is not a clear sequence of events, but that communicates a complex felt idea when it interacts with its audience. The dance may not appear logical; meaning gleaned from this more complex kind of narrative may emerge, be felt, be difficult or impossible to put into words. It is this kind of complex embodied narrative, experienced by performers and felt by audiences, that is at play when dance is able to contribute to communicating similarly complex scientific concepts or socioscientific issues.

Before delving farther into embodied narratives within actual dance and science education collaborations, it is worth introducing

Above:
Skin Deep, performed by All Change at Sadler's Wells, funded through the Wellcome Trust's Pulse scheme.
Tracey Fahy

the different models that are being used for this work to understand how these collaborations have actually been developed, as well as looking at the wider complexity of the relationship between dance and science collaborations (of which embodied narratives are a part).

A spectrum of intimacy

Dance artists and scientists have worked together in educational settings along a 'spectrum of intimacy', with the new, experimental approaches lying in the most intimate collaborations.

At the least intimate end are examples of encounters where science and dance enjoy a mild 'flirtation', where dance/movement presentation techniques have been used to enliven science teachers' practice. For example, classroom science bench demonstrations may be given a sense of art and suspense using movement flourishes and performance ideas. But if, for example, a science teacher merely demonstrates a chemical change with a well-timed dramatic pause followed by the exciting spectacle of vivid colour change and explosion, they are not exploiting the full potential of the dance–science interaction suggested in the phrase 'embodied narratives'.

Science and dance have come closer in projects designed to use performance and dance workshops to engage students in science, as well as offering professional development for classroom teachers in how to do this themselves – for instance, themed dance-based schemes of work focusing on science topics such as the water cycle or physical states of solid, liquid and gas. An example might involve students representing different energy states through the motions of molecules and their arrangement in space. Again, such workshops still do not exploit the full potential of the dance–science interaction in education, although they are fit for purpose.

Fraternising at the more intimate end of the spectrum, and featuring some of the most innovative current practices, are science and dance collaborations structured in mutually influential relationships, favouring strong discipline knowledge and experience within experts from each discipline. These science–dance–learning interactions are characterised by learning gains for parties within different disciplines, which result from the symbiosis between disciplines. Projects report these gains involving learning about learning, increasing understanding of where the sciences and the arts overlap in their approaches, and acknowledging the differences in order that they can be better understood and appropriately built upon. As such they are a promising culture for developing 'embodied narratives'.

An example of a project of this type is *Skin Deep*, a digital dance performance created by 58 young Londoners to explore the facts and fiction behind genetic science and its impact on society. All Change, in partnership with Sadler's Wells, worked with poets, dancers, musicians, digital artists and scientists to create digital artworks and choreography culminating in three digital dance performances. The project was supported by Dr Anand Saggar (a clinical geneticist) and Professor Alf Linney (a medical imaging physicist). This initially open-ended exploration of genetic science reported new learning regarding how dance, new media and scientific modes of enquiry can enlighten all those involved.

So what is going on within these more intimate kinds of collaboration? There are two key points here. First are the conceptualisations of creativity and process that science and dance bring to the melting pot, and how these fuel the symbiosis between disciplines. Second is the question of the kinds of narrative that dance can create around the socioscientific issues at hand, and how developing understanding of these contributes to new interpretations of ideas, and indeed to developing new approaches.

Above:
Dancers in *Left*, a theatre production by Double Vision supported by a Wellcome Trust Pulse award.

Different and yet the same: conceptualisations of creativity
The arts and sciences are tools for attempting to understand the world. It seems that those science–dance–learning collaborations that are likely to be the most successful in developing understanding will come through the symbiosis of disciplines, as well as the learning within disciplines. Nurturing this symbiosis appears to work best when the differences as well as the similarities between disciplines are acknowledged in practice, allowing for understanding of how science and dance can interact together to stimulate enquiring minds in young people. This is not an argument that has been empirically evidenced, but certainly emerged as a strong opinion within the Wellcome Trust's 2006 'Creative Encounters' seminar, which brought together arts and science collaborators to discuss such issues.

On one level there are obvious and tangible differences in how the arts and the sciences approach enquiry and the creative process because of their underlying epistemologies. Science is based on empirical enquiry about the material world, which yields instrumental and theoretical knowledge. The arts involve an aesthetic approach, at times allowing more space for ambiguity and uncertainty, and at others focused on critical reflection and the capture of valuable ideas. Within the school context, the arts acknowledge the existence of multiple perspectives that incorporate evaluative responses rather than the more illustrative and authoritative science knowledge (Chappell, 2006).

Despite these epistemological distinctions, on another level creative enquiry within these disciplines requires similar abilities, which include: being imaginative, risk-taking, question-posing, question-responding, self-determination, innovation, playfulness and immersion. These particular abilities are being investigated as the core features of what has been labelled 'possibility thinking', which it is argued lies at the heart of creativity (Craft *et al.*, in press). In particular, question-posing is emerging as the driving force of possibility thinking and creativity. Its relationship with the other features is currently being further investigated via empirical studies in schools. Although the two disciplines of dance and science both utilise these kinds of abilities, how they are manifested within the two domains is different.

Innervations (Hampshire Youth Dance Company working with a University of Southampton neuroscientist) provides a strong example of this (Parry, 2004). The project aimed to deepen understanding of the dynamic communication network of the brain through enquiry. In dance, students learned how to explore artistically, for example investigating how to represent the essence of neural networks in an aesthetic and embodied way (one approach was to connect the moving youth dancers using networks made from wool to represent the role of individual proteins at synapses during transmission). In neuroscience, scientifically grounded approaches were taken to students' learning (one exploration involved students taking pictures of neurons with a confocal microscope to aid understanding of conditions such as autism – for example, focusing on mirror neurons, which some studies have suggested are inactive in autistic children when they are attempting to understand emotions in others).

Above:
Participants in the *Innervations* project, supported with Wellcome Trust Pulse funding.

There was also cross-disciplinary learning, where the dance and science enquiry began to feed off each other as tools for attempting to understand the world, via abilities such as imagination, question-asking and risk-taking. Dance sequences grounded in scientific understanding raised questions and responses for the young dancers in process, and their audience in performance, around, for example, how autism might be better understood and perhaps ultimately treated. It also showed how difficult concepts might be more innovatively conceptualised in order to aid better public understanding of the value and contribution of science to everyday life.

How does dance create a narrative around socioscientific issues?

Given the complexity of the potential symbiosis between dance and science in educational collaborations, we now turn to one aspect of that symbiosis, the embodied narratives that dance can create around socioscientific issues.

As discussed at the beginning of the chapter, whether we experience dance as a performer or an audience member, there is something special about the encounter that we struggle to put into words. We are suddenly required to make meaning out of information through bodies. For some, this request to engage with embodied narratives is perhaps rare. In attempting to understand this, the work of Preston-Dunlop (1998) is particularly useful in explicating some of the mechanisms at play. In asking the question of how dance can create narrative and understanding around socioscientific issues it helps to be aware of the nexus of four elements at work within any dance piece: movement, performers, sound and space. Preston-Dunlop reminds us that choreographers connect the different elements in different ways – some integrating them, some juxtaposing them – developing different styles of connection.

Although dance communicates the choreographer's ideas, it also contains layers of meaning created by the participants in the event, including the performers and the audience. It is not a simple case of sending out a clear message to be received by one and all.

A further layer of complexity is added when we consider that often the kinds of dance within the science–dance–learning collaborations mostly fall within the 'creative' or 'contemporary' category. We are therefore not often dealing with pure dance genres such as Bharata Natyam (an Indian dance form), where each movement constitutes a sign that can be translated, or ballet, where, if we are educated in them, established codes communicate.

We are dealing with combinations of what Preston-Dunlop calls "unstable codes...aesthetic codes...behaviour codes" (1998, p. 10) with which the audience must actively engage to make their meaning.

A code will consist of carefully designed combinations of the four elements: different movements, performers, sounds and use of space. At times use of these codes will create embodied narratives that tell a story, but at other times they will create embodied narratives that are complex and not limited by narrative as linear storytelling. Within the dance, these embodied narratives are also combined with the choreographer's (and in this case scientist's and young people's) "attitudes, preferences, emphases, interests" (Preston-Dunlop, 1998, p. 14). As stated earlier, the dance may not appear logical; meaning gleaned from this combination of different embodied narratives, attitudes, preferences, emphases and interests emerges, and is felt, but is quite often difficult or impossible to put into words. Yet this does not mean it is not understood by performers and audience alike. It is felt and understood in an embodied way.

The Hampshire Dance University of Southampton's *Innervations* project can provide an example here. If we consider this dance piece in relation to the explanation above, we can begin to understand its power to communicate and interact with its audience via embodied narrative. We start to see how collaborations can move beyond the textbook of traditional science communication strategies to create something more personally and socially profound.

On one level, *Innervations*, the performance piece, was communicating the ideas about science – through the neural network model, using an interlaced network of wool fibres – that the dance artist, dancers and scientists wanted to get across, and to an extent telling a story to do so. Here the physical activity of individual proteins at synapses was being narrated as an embodied story for the audience, a sequence of quite tangible events using codes made up of components of the dance nexus (movement, space and performers in particular here). The codes being interpreted by the audience were, in this case, quite literal. Movement elements (actions of reaching and gently pulling to create tension in the network), space elements (the dimensions and properties of the wool fibre network containing the movement within a relatively tight and contained space on stage), and performer elements (the very young people who had been exploring the science dancing this particular embodied narrative) combined into codes that allowed the audience to better understand the sequenced activities of the communication network of the brain.

On another level the interactions and transactions of the live performance of *Innervations* were dealing with the personal and social issues that stem from malfunctions of the brain's communication network, such as autism and epilepsy. Developing this angle was perhaps the least story-based and most complex part of the embodied narrative. The disturbance of brain activity, and its experience outside and inside, at the heart of an epileptic episode were brought alive by young dancers performing in unison, using jolting extended fist movements, the other fist tight against the chest, within part red, part sickly yellow lighting. This sequence was not attempting to use the dancers to show what it might look like to see someone have an epileptic episode; it was entering into the realm of the more complex embodied narrative.

If we break the codes down, we can start to understand. I will describe to you part of how I interpret the codes within the description above and how it makes me feel. Fists jolting and held tight against chest are movements that induce in me anxiety, upset, disjointedness, a feeling that something is awry; part red, part sickly yellow lighting filling the space makes me feel nauseous, reminds me of the red of the inside of the brain and its faltering communication network; together these elements make me uncomfortable, especially being danced by such young people – could this happen to one of them, could it happen to me?

And we must remember that I am describing this in words; I cannot give you here the full complex embodied narrative and my embodied response to it, because when working at its best the interaction is embodied, and cannot be reduced to words. And another person may experience, decode and interpret the codes, containing the creative team's ideas made up of the elements of the nexus, in their own personally and culturally situated way, dependent on their own previous life experiences and attitudes.

This is just one small example drawn from the whole dance piece, but it explains the mechanisms of how, through the use of a variety of codes, and manipulation of the nexus, dance creates complex embodied narratives around socioscientific issues. To step closer towards fully explaining embodied narratives it is also vitally important to understand something of the aesthetic qualities and awareness at play.

Dance's unique integration of aesthetic qualities and awareness via the body into a way of knowing within an art form also informs meaning-making around scientific and socioscientific issues in the above examples. It is the aesthetic 'glue' between the components discussed above that is often contributing to new interpretations of ideas, and indeed developing new approaches. But, even within dance education, there have been recent calls for the re-evaluation and rejuvenation of the aesthetic within education (e.g. Bannon and Sanderson, 2000), as there is a fear that it is being subsumed by other current educational priorities.

Smith-Autard (2002) helps us to understand what aesthetic qualities, awareness and understanding in dance involve. She argues that aesthetic education is essentially an education of feeling and that "aesthetic perception, though probably something with which we are all endowed, needs, like other kinds of perception, to be nurtured and developed...we need to learn to attend to contained qualities in dance rather than the mere physicalities of bodies in action" (p. 33). The expressive aesthetic qualities in dance are emergent features of the sensory qualities of the dance, as can be seen in the very short example of the epileptic episode from *Innervations* detailed above.

Smith-Autard also draws on Gibson (in Abbs, 1989, p. 58), whose words are especially pertinent to this discussion:

> Feelings show us the limits of our language. They bring home to us that language is not omnicompetent; for we know far more than we can say. It is when we try to put into words our feelings, when we attend to explore our inner states (states that vividly and significantly exist, have reality and are of profound consequences for action) that the gap between language and experience is starkly exposed. It is such moments we must turn to poets and artists, not scientists, for genuine illumination... Feelings...are processes not products...they are grasped and intuited only in their moment of experiencing...It is with this present, shared, experienced, nature of emotions in mind that we return to the question of the education of feeling...

It is this complex understanding of feeling within art, not anything so simplistic as the expression of emotion, that is at play in the best science–dance–learning collaborations. Dance artists are highly skilled in this 'education of feeling' and traditionally undertake it by engaging young people in the three interrelated processes of creating, performing and viewing in order to generate an appreciation of dance as art (e.g. Smith-Autard, 2002). The young people in projects such as *Innervations* will have had the opportunity to engage as creators, performers and viewers generating, embodying and receiving/interacting with complex ideas, feelings, emotions and narratives about neuroscience, related conditions and the connected socioscientific issues.

Within these collaborations, young people are therefore experiencing the best of both worlds. They are able to engage with the 'illumination' possible through the ways of knowing in dance and other art forms, as well as simultaneously engaging with the scientific way of knowing and its product. They are able to work to use the synthesis of dance and science in attempting to understand the world.

Conclusion and moving forward

The idea of a creative educational collaboration between a scientist and a dance artist is one that is not so far-fetched. There is growing opinion that when dance and science interact in intimate educational collaborations that acknowledge discipline similarities and differences, there is the potential for learning within disciplines, as well as a symbiosis between disciplines that leads to wider learning. One part of this symbiosis is the way in which dance can create powerful embodied narratives and make meaning around socioscientific issues.

Fundamental to the development of these narratives and their interpretation by performers and audiences is understanding from within dance, regarding the complex mechanisms for making dance and its constituent codes, integrated with aesthetic understanding and awareness. Embodied narratives are difficult to understand for those not accustomed to gleaning and interpreting information through the body. Practitioners need to raise the profile of what it means to understand in an embodied way if this work is to go farther. A science educator who had been employed in a collaborative project to lead post-dance-performance discussions commented that people don't always 'get' the dance and they need to talk to fully understand. There is no question that this supplementary talk is very valuable, and critical discussion is a strong component of dance-making and the dance community. But we need to better understand the embodied in these collaborations to re-address the balance. It would be beneficial to collaborations if the default position was not immediate attempts to translate the embodied into the spoken, but acceptance that the embodied is as valid a form of understanding.

We must also work to experience embodied narratives on a scale from sequential storytelling to the communication of complex felt ideas that may not have a straightforward narrative form – and, in fact, acknowledge that both these things may be going on simultaneously. The range of embodied narratives have the potential to tell a story or sequence of events to explain the science. But they can also stimulate the performers and audience to engage in questions grounded in feelings about, for example, what it means to experience epilepsy from the inside and the outside, how we might be able to understand autism and its dislocation and why this is important. As two epigenetics/dance project students (the first an audience member, the second a performer) put it: "compared to if you're learning epigenetics in a textbook, if you see it [the dance performance] you understand it more, about the shapes and stuff. It's much better than looking in a book because you see it happening," and "'cos it's about you; why not know about it".

Finally, it is important to maintain wider questioning about what is going on within collaborations. The focus on embodied narratives within this chapter has shone the spotlight most strongly on dance products and their interaction with the audience, but we need to continue to debate about the contribution of the dance process, particularly in terms of how it interacts with the scientific processes in symbiosis.

In relation to this, it is important to pay attention to complementarities and tensions within collaborations: process needs space alongside product; story needs space alongside complex felt ideas; the known needs space alongside the unknown; bodily expression needs space alongside verbal expression. And I would suggest that each pair's role needs acknowledging within both disciplines. This is difficult, but it is often dealing with challenges such as this that sparks new approaches, some of which are already inherent within the strongest science–dance collaborations.

1 This chapter is focusing on collaborations between scientists and dance artists that develop young people's arts work engaging with science. It is not attempting to deal with current debates and questions about epistemology and meaning-making from within the developing discipline of dance science.

Bibliography

Bannon F, Sanderson P. Experience every moment: aesthetically significant dance education. Research in Dance Education 2000;1(1):9–26.

Chappell K. Creativity within late primary age dance education: unlocking expert specialist dance teachers' conceptions and approaches. PhD thesis. Laban: London; 2006. http://kn.open.ac.uk/public/document.cfm?documentid=8627 [accessed 9 January 2008].

Craft A et al. Developing creative learning through possibility thinking with children aged 3–7. In A Craft et al. (eds). Creative Learning and How We Document it. Stoke-on-Trent: Trentham Books; in press.

Parry S (ed.). Pulse: Youth arts inspired by biomedical science. London: Wellcome Trust; 2004.

Preston-Dunlop V. Looking at Dances: A choreological perspective on choreography. London: Verve; 1998.

Smith-Autard J. The Art of Dance in Education. London: A & C Black; 2002.

Stinson SW. My body/myself: lessons from dance education. In L Bresler (ed.). Knowing Bodies, Moving Minds: Towards embodied teaching and learning. London: Kluwer Academic; 2004.

The pedagogy and performance of Sci:dentities

Catherine McNamara
Alison Rooke

Society dictates that people fall into one of two sexual identities: male or female. For some people, though, sex is not so clear-cut. They may have an intersex condition or feel that there is a mismatch between their biological sex and the gender they perceive themselves to be. *Catherine McNamara* and *Alison Rooke* describe here a project in which a group of transsexual and transgendered young people were able to explore – and challenge – the biological determinants and medical understanding of sex and gender, and also to express their perceptions through performance. As well as helping the young people to make more sense of their sexed and gendered identities, the project enabled them to communicate a picture of transgendered lived experience that goes beyond limited scientific and medical descriptions.

Above:
'Untitled' artwork by James,
Sci:dentity exhibition,
November 2006.

Introduction

Gender is everywhere. Everyone has a personal relationship to gender and expresses gender in complex ways. In this project, multiple stories were explored and articulated by trans and non-trans young people and those engaged in working with them in a variety of settings, by way of cultivating more intelligent approaches to gender diversity. This chapter draws on the particular experiences of the young people and practitioners who worked on the Sci:dentity project, based at the Central School of Speech and Drama in London from March 2006 to March 2007. It focuses on the issues raised by the personal and collective journeys taken in the process of engaging with the science of sex and gender within the project. By offering accounts of the personal narratives explored by the young participants during the life of the project and beyond, we aim to debate the role of creativity and pedagogy in science and arts education with young people. We ask why and how those personal stories are told as part of a journey in which young people develop their understandings of their own identity.

The Sci:dentity project

At the heart of this project was the question 'What is the science of sex and gender?' There were two main phases: firstly a series of arts workshops were provided for a group of 18 young transgendered and transsexual people[1] aged between 15 and 22 who were living their sex and gender with a degree of complexity; and secondly, a series of 16 outreach workshops in various settings. The latter workshops reached a variety of audiences including school and college students, trainee drama teachers, young people including LGBT[2] youth, teachers, youth workers, arts practitioners, educationalists, activists and those working in the area of equalities and diversity policy and delivery. A documentary film about the arts workshops was shown in the outreach workshops with the aim of communicating the lessons of the project and the life experiences of the participants to a wide range of people who were most often coming across the notion and the lived reality of transgender for the first time. The outreach workshops involved predominantly non-trans young people under 22 years of age from all over the UK. The project drew on scientific explanations of sex and gender differences such as differences in the brain, hormones and their effect on behaviour, chromosomes and their function, hormonal and surgical sex reassignment, as well as the moral and ethical issues that are raised by sex reassignment. In questioning the authority of science and medicine, it became possible to make use of new knowledge through art by exploring how sex and gender are understood by both transsexual and transgendered people and in society in general.

Transgendered people live in a world where there are commonsense understandings of what makes a man or woman. Biological sex at birth is commonly perceived to be the matter that makes sex and gender 'real'. These understandings of the authenticity of biology tend to marginalise transgendered people, trivialise their self-understandings and undermine their struggles for recognition. The Sci:dentity project gave young transgendered people an opportunity to share their experiences, to experiment and to critically explore their own and societal understandings of gender.

The first phase of the project (the arts workshops with young trans people) consisted of three working groups – film, live performance and visual art – which then produced several pieces of artwork in response to the question 'What is the science of sex and gender?' This phase of the project culminated in an exhibition and performance, which was attended by an audience that included families, friends, members of the LGBT communities, academics and representatives from a range of organisations. The workshop process was filmed and subsequently produced as a short documentary film that linked the first and second phases of the project.

The science of sex and gender: getting personal

While the majority of individuals take the materiality of 'sex' as a given, on closer inspection it is in fact difficult to pinpoint exactly where sex lies in the body and how it is determined. Sex is defined in many ways. When assigning a newborn baby with its sexed identity, doctors take very few factors into consideration. If we appear male, i.e. have male genitalia, we are labelled 'male'. Biochemical sex is defined by the absence of the Y chromosome. The main sex hormones are testosterone and oestrogen; they make profound changes to our physiology but do chemicals make us who we are? The project was an opportunity to interrogate the perceived certainties of the science of sex and critique them through art, so challenging, for example, the presumption that one's physical sex necessarily correlates with chromosomal sex. Raising such questions affected sexual identity and self-image:

> I think once you shed the ideal images of what a man and woman should be...it's easier to accept your own body, when you realise there is no clear line. It's like OK, I'm a short, unusual guy, and there's lots of them about and not all of them are even trans! The challenge becomes less of an internal battle (mind versus matter), more of a process of getting the recognition of who you are. (Participant R)

Transsexuality then, might be viewed as a trope for the relationship between scientific and medical worlds, and all sexed identities. Just as the worlds of science and medicine continue to develop their knowledge of sex and transsexuality, trans people themselves will need to carry out their research into the science of sex. If the young participants in this project choose to undergo a medical transition these are the bodies of knowledge they will potentially have to navigate. Through each transsexual person's life s/he will encounter various medical specialists in the fields of endocrinology, surgery and psychiatry. Growing awareness of transsexuality means that increasing numbers of people are identifying as trans and becoming involved in trans as a social identity rather than a medical diagnosis of a psychiatric disorder. Trans people are taking part in a range of support networks, getting involved in activism and wishing to change their sex at a younger age. Simultaneously, medical practitioners are faced with making difficult ethical decisions when negotiating their treatment of a young trans person. Guidance is contained in the *Harry Benjamin Standards of Care for Gender Identity Disorders* (2001), suggesting caution with regard to the diagnosis and treatment of young people. Concerns include decisions whether to administer only reversible treatments such as hormone blockers to the trans adolescent rather than irreversible treatments such as hormone administration and surgery.

While the medical profession tends to delay treating young trans people, there also exists a practice of self-diagnosis and self-medication among young trans people who are opting out of the existing psychiatric and medical framework for understanding transsexuality. Furthermore, increased global communication has led to drugs (steroids) and surgical procedures (cosmetic surgery) becoming widely available to those that can gain access to and afford them. It is at this nexus, between medical discourses of transsexuality and a growing understanding of trans as a social identity, that this project lies.

Pedagogical strategies: undoing the science of sex

The workshops of the first phase of the project addressed the scientific and ethical issues surrounding trans identities using a range of pedagogical strategies, and included three sessions specifically planned to develop the young people's knowledge and understanding of biomedical subject matter. The first 'science lesson' during weekend one of the project was a presentation by the Gender Identity Research and Education Society (GIRES), which summarised existing scientific understandings of sex and gender. This science session offered a detailed explanation of sex cell activity, the relationship between chromosomes and hormones as well as how they affect the body and brain, and included information on atypical sex differentiation, chromosomal anomalies and intersex conditions. Following the presentation the young participants debated the science of sex, questions were asked and the group reflected on the information offered.

During the second weekend of the project the participants learned a number of interview techniques and went on to formulate sets of questions in preparation for further researching the science of sex and gender with an endocrinologist, a GP and gender specialist, an older trans man (and artist), and an older trans woman (and academic). The participants then conducted these interviews over the subsequent weekends. The questions they asked demonstrated significant understandings of the science of sex and gender and curiosity about the relationship between the various models of sex and gender employed by psychiatrists, endocrinologists and GPs.

The interview with the endocrinologist included questions about the extent to which behaviour and qualities associated with femininity and masculinity are due to hormone levels, such as: "Is it true that testosterone enhances qualities that are considered stereotypically male, for example loving/tenderness decreases, and attention span shortens?" The participants conducting this interview also asked medically sophisticated questions about hormones: "If you take testosterone how and when does it affect your oestrogen production and levels?" These questions revealed a well-developed understanding of the kinds of scientific knowledge a trans person will need when navigating the science of sex and gender if they choose to take a medical journey and transition. In this process each medical professional will have quite specific models for understanding sex and gender. The participants were aware of, and somewhat critical of, these differing models and the potential influence on their lives. This was apparent in the following question to the GP: "What (if any) is the relationship between a GP, psychiatrist and an endocrinologist when treating a trans person? Do your professional frameworks for understanding gender and (trans)sex overlap?", and to the endocrinologist: "What is the relationship between theories of hormones and theories of brain sex? Does endocrinology endorse 'brain sex' theories?"

Some of the work that the young people were producing was a critique of a science that produces a distinctly gender-binaried world. The GIRES session examined the neurological research evidence base for arguing that there are differences in male and female brains (i.e. trans people may have a male brain in a female body and vice versa). Although this thesis offers a case for understanding a transsexual experience, some of the young people felt that this approach reified distinct male and female sexes. This participant who identifies as genderqueer was critical of this science of binaries, even as an attempt to explain trans:

> I hope that when I die they look at my brain and find that it's neither male nor female and then I'll feel…justified for all of this. I don't think science has a good relationship with trans people, I'm wary of things being biological and 'curing' us – just let us do what we need to be happy in our own skin and everyday lives, just like everyone else. (Participant P)

The interview schedules devised by the young people, and the responses from the medical specialists and the two older trans people, gave the group an opportunity to discuss their specific questions and concerns. For some of the participants the investigation into the existing state of scientific knowledge revealed how little is actually known about trans and the potential long-term effects of hormone therapy, as the following statement illustrates: "I did learn some new stuff. I also thought about some old stuff in a new way. I learnt a lot about the lack of scientific/ medical understanding about sex, or rather, that understanding became less of a concept and more of a reality. It has driven me to learn more about sex and intersex" (Participant R). Within the process of responding creatively to science, young transgendered people were both telling their own stories and interacting with each other's. They have their own histories and experiences, which were profoundly transformed through challenging the science, their perceptions and perceptions of them in society, their sense of community in working together, and indeed what creativity means to them.

Nicholson (2005) suggests there can be a "productive consonance" between what some arts practitioners separate out as a product/ process binary or division, e.g. the processes of making meaning are as creative, interesting and productive as the point at which a piece of work is shown (p. 4). There was a clear sense of the compulsion to tell one's story among the group of young people working on the project, and the telling of stories was part of the process of coming to an understanding. The act of articulating an account of personal experience to another produced meaning and understanding for the individuals involved, which then led into the production of artistic work. So this was a multiple process. As a staff team, we understood that the act of storytelling within sessions is not straightforward: not everyone wants to tell theirs, or feels the compulsion to make their personal experience public. We were interested in finding ways for individuals to mediate the extent to which the synthesis of scientific discourses and personal experiences became 'public', either within the sessions among their peers or as part of an exhibition of work derived from these explorations. Our responsibility as arts practitioners was to provide choices in terms of methods of exploration, modes of expression and media of communication such that participants were able to use autobiography and draw on personal stories, but in a way that wouldn't expose their vulnerability, nor even lead them to perform something they might later regret in terms of revealing the personal in a public arena. In this project, for example, it was likely that a participant's relationship to their image as it appears within the documentary film would shift and change over time – the consent they gave during the project had to be flexible enough to accommodate a change of mind, were one of the young people to 'go stealth' in future and object to their being shown as transgendered. We will return to this point later in relation to appearing as trans within mainstream settings.

That the workshops were focused on making art for an exhibition was clear from the outset. We were all working towards that event and its audience. We talked about the exhibition in the pre-project publicity and from day one of the workshops. However, there were individuals in the group who only fully understood at a late stage that the audience would be other people, not just us as a group viewing each other's work. Some of the participants were working in a more insular, processual way, exploring their own stories in the company of others, as distinct from selecting aspects of their personal narrative to create work as a way to say something to an audience. There are differences here, and while on the whole a 'productive consonance' was evident, we surely restricted or stifled certain processes too. Understanding the complexity of the process of joining a group and exploring a question rooted in the discipline of science, using the arts as a medium of expression for one's personal responses to that question, and mediating those responses for audiences were critical to the quality of the participants' engagement with this project.

The understanding and critical awareness that was gained in the process was developed and shaped over the four residential weekends. The arts workshops asked the participants to express and explore their understandings of the biomedicine of sex and transsexuality through a range of creative practices. These included film making, photography, performance, painting, sculpture, creative writing and music. The structured nature of the project and the involvement of the various specialists who contributed, alongside the dialogue and peer education that the project facilitated, created opportunities for learning. This was contrasted with the difficulties of relying on the internet when researching information about trans issues. The following excerpt that two participants wrote for the 'zine,[3] produced as part of the exhibition, encapsulates some of the difficulties of researching medical and personal trans narratives on the internet:

I've been trying to research effects of T [testosterone] but the internet is, as usual, a minefield of conflicting information. In fact, one site went on about how it increases risks of breast cancer if I don't get 'em chopped off (which I wouldn't, they're teeny anyhow), and another one said the exact opposite. Oh, and the internet doesn't really say much about hormones etc., which is where I keep on going in my head with this, every time I think about it. Scary. (Participant A)

I consider myself a newly 'discovered' transboy as I only came out in February of this year. I am pretty new to everything, all the new terms and information makes my head hurt. Most of my research has been through various TG sites on the internet. Different websites say different things, but nothing beats meeting a trans person in person and talking to them. I got to do that this weekend and I am very happy I met the guys here, as it helps me convert text and websites into real life experience. (Participant H)

One of the central themes in learning about the science of sex and gender was the development of a critique of medical ethics in relation to the diagnosis and treatment of transsexuality as a disorder. Many participants were coming together to celebrate their transgendered identities and express their creativity as trans people, as opposed to keeping this aspect of their identity hidden. This identity-positive environment existed in contrast to the medical diagnosis of trans as a type of disorder or dysphoria and the associated ethical dilemmas:

> I've pondered how gender and transition relate with other body modifications (piercings, tattoos, cosmetic surgery) because to get your tits enlarged you just need money, but to get them cut off you need a gender shrink. That's bloody weird! Where do you draw the line between someone who wants non-genital cosmetic surgery and someone who wants genital cosmetic surgery? Why is one more of a problem for society than the other? Why does society require that we have an either/or gender? (Participant A)

> I don't particularly think science has much of a place, because while the GIRES woman was on about 'brain sex', the endocrinologist didn't think much of it. I think there's got to be more evidence over a longer period of time for there to be a proper link established. However I think it could be dangerous if a 'trans gene' or such was found, because then there's always the possibility of parents wanting to have a 'normal' child and abort a child solely because of its 'trans' status. (Participant C)

> How do you feel about the rightness and wrongness of a person's transition? How do you feel about having the responsibility of making decisions about a person's transition process? (Question formulated by participants for a GP and gender specialist)

Re-presenting the invisible

The nature of education, within and outside of the curriculum, becomes significant in relation to the conversations, debates and activities that took place within this project. These kinds of conversation are not happening in schools. They could be happening in the biology curriculum but they do not. They could be happening in the citizenship or the personal, social and health education curricula but they do not. Consequently a range of negative impacts arise such as bullying related to gender, and young gender-variant people withdrawing from the learning process because they feel they are not represented within the curriculum so are marginalised, with a range of negative consequences.

Current research carried out by Stephen Whittle *et al.* (2007) shows that young trans people are suffering high levels of violence and abuse. This report, which reviews existing research on trans peoples' experience, found that 48 per cent of respondents had been victims of assault, including sexual assault and rape, and 78 per cent had experienced verbal harassment. Whittle's research shows that many of those people working with young trans people such as school teachers, school psychologists and social workers have not received training in trans awareness and perpetuate negative attitudes and transphobia.

Trans youth are clearly aware of the limits of a curriculum that does not do justice to their experience and perpetuates ignorance about trans lives:

> Our school pretends to be all-inclusive and everything 'cause we had a lesson on sex and relationships and all that sort of thing. The only thing we got was a reassurance that homosexuals aren't paedophiles. That's as close as it was. I've still got the piece of paper and it says it. (Participant E)

I've got to say, that if this was done in sex education in year 6,
and in year 9 and all that, people would understand it more, and
therefore they wouldn't be as afraid of it. Therefore there'd be
less bullying. But, transsexualism, and homosexuality, are just
seemingly pushed under the carpet. And it's you know, sex
education is just 'men have willies, women have fannies' and…
and that's how babies are made (Participant R)

The Sci:dentity project offered a learning environment akin to a
mainstream school setting, in that it was structured, with clear
session aims and objectives. The science and arts 'curriculum
content' of this project directly engaged with the participants as
learners in a way that enabled them to see themselves as part of the
discourses explored. The Sci:dentity project, through the public
exhibition of work, the documentary film screenings and the phase
two outreach sessions, demonstrates that it is possible to represent
and explore complex gendered identities and that non-trans young
people in education are interested in debating and making sense of
gender normativity. During the outreach sessions, non-trans
young people demonstrated a sophisticated awareness of the
cultural work that gender norms do, and some of the ways that they
also find them difficult. The outreach sessions drew parallels
between these experiences to deepen the participants'
understandings of trans. However, the experiences of the young
trans participants in phase one clearly demonstrates that they feel
marginalised and excluded from mainstream statutory settings in
an educational climate that does not provide teaching on trans
identities, or awareness-raising regarding trans phobia and
bullying:

Schools don't teach about being transgendered or transsexual.
Schools don't even talk about being gay. How much happier I
would have been if I could have known earlier? How much easier
would it make it for so many children and young people if they
could know they weren't alone? How many lives might have

been saved if only, if only, someone in authority would acknowledge the necessity for young people to know that it's okay to be different, to be gender variant? How many people are still searching for an answer and not finding it? How many will never find it? (Catherine, weblog question)

Some of the participants who felt reluctant about distribution of the DVD that documents the project are testament to their enduring concerns about being 'out' as trans in educational settings.

Individual and collective journeys

One of the key features of the Sci:dentity project was the way in which the participants engaged in scientific creativity. Rather than being passive recipients of science education, science and art were things that they did and things they made use of in the workshop space, and beyond. At the heart of this process was a biographical narrating of being transsexual and transgendered, which often contrasted with the current medical diagnostic version of transsexuality. In this process the participants were able to communicate the far-reaching consequences and difficulties of living as a young trans person while simultaneously developing individual and collective critiques of the science and medicinal practices that reproduce the coherence of sex and gender.

Almost all of the participants had done considerable (mostly web-based) research into available medical and scientific information about sex and gender generally and transsexuality specifically in the process of self-diagnosis and seeking out peer support. Although this demonstrates resourcefulness, it has limitations, as the participants' discussion of this earlier illustrates. Four of the participants were already living in relation to medical understandings of sex and gender, as they were either being referred to, or were already clients of, gender identity clinics. On their personal journeys they had already encountered a range of medical practitioners such as endocrinologists and psychiatrists in the process of being diagnosed as 'gender dysphoric'.[4] By participating in the project they had an opportunity to develop an informed critique of current medical models of trans-identities. As the following illustrates:

> What do you feel you have learnt about the science of sex and gender so far in the project? (Catherine, weblog question)

> Where do I start! As I already said, lots of terminology and facts about hormones, brain sex, and scientific points of view in relation to transsexuality – but more importantly and more interestingly, how science is a social construct (albeit a long-established one) which is always changing and adapting to personal experiences and social movements. And if it isn't, IT SHOULD BE! So not to always accept science as gospel! (Participant A)

The participants questioned popular conceptions, such as those found in television documentaries, of transsexuality being a process of having a 'sex change' or making a journey from one sex to another. This is a process often understood as having a distinct beginning, middle and end. In this narrative the trans person is constructed as being someone in the 'wrong body', who, in the process of undergoing psychiatry will be diagnosed as gender dysphoric, undergo hormonal treatment, have surgery and arrive at the destination of their new sex. These representations and life narratives do not leave room for the possibility of being transgendered, of identifying as neither male nor female, or both male and female, and the possibility of stopping at a point between A and B. The young people's response to the 'authority' of scientific knowledge and medical professionals in relation to trans identities was clearly communicated in the Sci:dentity exhibition, which showed the ways in which trans people are human, working against both a medical model of trans and the more sensational representations of trans people in the media. Early sessions that focused on representations of sex and gender in the media and art made it apparent that art offers an ambiguous space where meaning is produced through creative practices and the various readings of those representations. This ambiguity was utilised in the use of autobiography, and the artwork produced nuanced representations of trans. The themes of the exhibition reflected the young people's concerns, passions and experiences. These included 'passing',[5] relationships with family, friends, coming out, feeling different from the 'norm' and negotiating places such as clubs, bars, toilets and trains. The artwork focused on the participants' own experience of transsexual and transgender identities as a variety of different journeys and potential life trajectories.

Early discussions about the exhibition led to the creation of the 'grey area', an area in the exhibition, which worked to undo gender binaries. Installations included a large toilet cubicle covered in comments that the participants had heard when they have been seen to be entering the 'wrong' toilet, a collage titled 'Buying into Gender' showing gendered consumer goods, a video installation playing with clothes and gender stereotypes, and a sculpture of gender stereotypical clothes that had been subject to some modification. Similarly, the artistic space opened up an alternative to scientific paradigms. Rather than sex being a matter of certainty found in verifiable evidence of scientific facts, art offered the opportunity to communicate the humanity of trans, with dignity and pathos. The performances and artwork worked against the 'freakshow' presentations popular in the contemporary talkshow genre (Gamson, 1998) and instead portrayed the consequences of living in relation to the stigma that trans people encounter due to popular misconceptions of transsexuality that these representations perpetuate:

> Unlike a television documentary the bare facts of human experience could not be switched off or ignored. We felt like

participants in the event, particularly in the grey area where images, sounds and experiences assault the senses. Performers laid themselves bare with experiences it hurt to imagine, sending us away still thinking and talking about what we'd seen long into the next week. Indeed, some of the performed items sizzled with a mixture of comedy and tragedy worthy of professional pieces. Clearly the group has real talent. Because the show is built on autobiography the audience can go some way to experiencing how it is to be a trans youth, with the inevitable move away from the 'Trisha Show' mentality of thinking trans people are freaks. The whole evening toyed with our prejudices and inevitably left us feeling difference must be celebrated and affirmed in the beautifully positive way the group itself was able to do. (Emailed response from two guests after attending the Sci:dentity exhibition)

This critique of these popular and medical conceptions of trans is perhaps best illustrated in some of the vignettes that make up the short film made by the project participants titled *Trans Journeys*, which was screened at the exhibition. In the short autobiographical clips the participants offer their own accounts of their journeys. These are journeys that do not necessarily follow an A to B process and that embrace *being* trans, i.e. that trans is an identity in and of itself, in a way that intelligently and playfully challenges the popular understandings of the temporality of trans lives. This was demonstrated throughout the project but illustrated here in the work of Participant N. At the start of the process, after weekend one, N expressed some ambivalence about the science of sex presented that weekend: "the most challenging aspect of the weekend for me was the science talk and the thoughts and feelings it always evokes in me when biology is mentioned". By the end of the creative engagement phase he had used these feelings to question the authority of science based on his experience of approaching his GP to ask to be referred to a gender identity clinic. As a result, he made a piece of work reflecting this encounter with medical understandings of sex and gender. He explains what happened:

My doctor called it 'the gender determination department'. When I said to him 'no it's the gender identity clinic', he didn't know any of the doctors' names, so later on I wrote 'To [name of doctor]' on it.

He then describes his experience of the appointment:

So I talked to him about things and he immediately turned away from me and listened to me, but pretended to fiddle about on his computer and stuff, and then eventually he wrote this: 'This 22 years old asked me to refer her as she has not been feeling fully female, as felt more male gender in her physical and mental activities. Her menarche started late 14, and her sexual organs showed reasonable development. She denies any hirstuitism, would you kindly see her for further investigations.'

Participant N had a frustrating experience with this initial approach to his GP. From the content of the letter, it seems that the GP has no knowledge of transsexualism and may have referred N for investigations into whether he was in fact intersexed. N decided to use this frustrating experience as a creative resource. He worked with the content of the letter, with the intention of reworking it until it reflected his self-understanding, as he explains here discussing his idea for his short film:

I'm going to read [the letter his GP wrote] out and change it and change it and change it until it's completely relevant to who I am, not to how my doctor with his ignorance had to write it. I'm going to adapt it and change it 3 or 4 times, each time changing it a bit more to suit. There will be a progression; 'cause that's what a transition is; from what's not acceptable/not real, to a better place. ...

There's going to be a voice over with imagery; shaving on a beard then plucking it off. I'll be playing with gender visually. A close-up of me is enough to make people question gender. If that's on there as a visual the letter isn't isolated. It will be with visuals; that's important because if I'm in the video shaving you can be more challenging.

Participant N then went on to make his short film, which incorporated the letter and visual images to retell this story and articulate his experience. The Sci:dentity participants communicated the variety and complexity of the journeys that people take, the self-understandings that lay within these various journeys and the particular ways in which the NHS mediates this process.

Conclusions

Judith Butler, who philosophises on the cultural meanings and consequences of sex and gender, reminds us that:

> [T]he critique of gender norms must be situated within the context of lives as they are lived and must be guided by the questions of what maximises the possibilities for a livable life, what minimises the possibility of an unbearable life, or indeed, social or literal death. (2006, p. 7)

The Sci:dentity project was an opportunity to critique gender norms and the apparent scientific certainties of sex that were situated in the complex context of young trans people's lives as they are lived every day. The Sci:dentity project offered space and time, however temporary and short, where young trans participants could experience support and respect and the possibility of what Butler describes as "a livable life". It explored gendered and creative expression, scientific and popular cultural narratives of sex, gender, and the meanings of transsexuality and transgender, and provided an opportunity to re-imagine and re-tell one's life narrative beyond simplistic accounts of being 'in the wrong body'. Since the end of the project participants have continued to be involved in gender pedagogy, whether on a personal level with their families, friends and associates, through creative activities such as producing music, 'zines, paintings and pamphlets, or as part of formal learning or political activity, such as being engaged in grassroots trans organisations. Four Sci:dentity youth, together with two of the Sci:dentity team, became involved with the Department of Health's Sexual Orientation and Gender Identity Advisory Group (SOGIAG). This group was established as part of the Department's Equality and Human Rights team, which seeks to make healthcare in the UK more accessible to LGBT people, and this link has resulted in the publication of *A Guide for Young Trans People in the UK* (2007).

1 Throughout this chapter certain terms are used that need explanation for the sake of clarity. Trans is used in this report to include transsexual and transgendered. Transsexual is a medical term used to refer to a person who identifies as a gender different from that which they were assigned at birth. Transsexuals usually undergo a medical process of sex reassignment through the use of surgery and the administration of hormones. Transgender is a more colloquial term used to describe a person who feels that the gender assigned to them at birth is not a correct or complete description of what they feel. Transgender can be used to describe a wide range of gender expressions, which are a variation from the norms of society (for example including masculine or 'butch' women, feminine men, cross-dressers). Genderqueer is also a colloquial or community term that describes someone who identifies as a gender other than 'man' or 'woman', or someone who identifies as neither, both, or some combination thereof. In relation to the male/female, genderqueer people generally identify as more 'both/and' or 'neither/nor', rather than 'either/or'. Some genderqueer people may identify as a gender and some see it as a third gender in addition to the traditional two. The commonality is that all genderqueer people are ambivalent about the notion that there are only two genders in the world.

2 LGBT is an acronym for lesbian, gay, bisexual and trans.

3 'Zine is shorthand for magazine, usually produced on a low budget and in a low-tech format. The Sci:dentity 'zine is now available at the Women's Library, London.

4 Gender dysphoria is the medical diagnosis for a transsexual person. Trans people do not generally embrace this term.

5 'Passing' refers to being read in public as the gender one feels oneself to be, and/or not being read as being trans. Hence an FTM (female-to-male) man will wish to 'pass' as male. There is considerable debate within trans communities about the term passing, as it implies being read as what one is not. There is also considerable debate regarding whether one should wish to pass rather than being a visible trans person.

Bibliography

Butler. J Undoing Gender. London: Routledge; 2006.

Gamson J. Freaks Talk Back: Tabloid talk shows and sexual nonconformity. Chicago: University of Chicago Press; 1998.

Gendered Intelligence and GALYIC. A Guide for Young Trans People in the UK Department of Health; 2007. www.dh.gov.uk/en/Publicationsandstatistics/Publications/PublicationsPolicyAndGuidance/DH_074258 [accessed 14 January 2008].

Harry Benjamin Standards of Care for Gender Identity Disorders. Sixth Edition. The Harry Benjamin International Gender Dysphoria Association; 2001.

Nicholson H. Applied Drama: The gift of theatre. Hampshire: Palgrave Macmillan; 2005.

Rooke A. The Sci:dentity Project Evaluation Report: Phases 1 and 2. Goldsmiths, University of London, Centre for Urban and Community Research; 2006. www.goldsmiths.ac.uk/cucr/pdf/sciidentevalu.pdf [accessed 14 January 2008].

Rooke A. The Sci:dentity Project Evaluation Report: Phases 3 and 4. Goldsmiths, University of London, Centre for Urban and Community Research; 2007. www.goldsmiths.ac.uk/cucr/pdf/sci-report-34.pdf [accessed 14 January 2008].

Whittle S et al. Engendered Penalties: Transgender and transsexual people's experiences of inequality and discrimination. West Yorkshire: Communities and Local Government Publications; 2007. www.pfc.org.uk/files/EngenderedPenalties.pdf [accessed 14 January 2008].

Conclusions

The aim of this book is to document and to try to understand how science and the arts can shed new light on each other when juxtaposed in fresh ways. The book focuses on how this happens within educational contexts in which approaches to both young people's science and arts education respond to emerging ideas about what it might mean to be a citizen in the 21st century.

The contributors to the book are all working in different contexts and are driven by a range of motivations. Arts educators or youth workers may be inspired by a fresh engagement with a topic they had not studied since they were at school. They might regard the science as unusual material for building on students' facility with a particular art form, be driven by socio-political beliefs or countless other motivating factors. Science educators may be particularly concerned with producing the next generation of elite research scientists. They may hope to pass on their personal passion for science as a rewarding body of knowledge. They may feel they are contributing to a future scientifically literate workforce which will ensure national economic competitiveness or see science education as key to students' political empowerment. Various combinations of these and other motivations may inform the broad range of practices.

There are also simple practical differences between the educational approaches appropriate within the structures and institutions of formal education and arts or science activities where young people participate in their own time. Given this diversity it could never be proposed that all the challenges facing science education for young people could be met by interdisciplinary collaboration or creative activity. Yet these intertwining strands suggest that creative encounters may become an established feature of the formal or informal education landscape. Hence, in the interests of stimulating further discussion, it might be worth laying out in a clear though admittedly reductive format, what some of the lessons learned by the practitioners writing in this book might be boiled down to.

The art of creative encounters

Creative encounters will often involve non-linear thinking, moving around a problem and looking at it from different perspectives. The introduction to this book and the start of the conclusion have circled the same issues and had to tread with trepidation on territory outside the natural habitat of its editors, roaming across politics, management, science, education, art and ethics. This is a risky business. Similarly, projects that cross disciplines are likely to require more effort, time, energy and maybe resources than work which remains within domain-specific patterns of interaction.

Creative encounters will therefore sometimes fail. The accounts in this book may understandably give an impression that interdisciplinary education always transforms learning and leaves a warm glow. Mostly it does, but not every artist will be able to develop a successful working relationship with a scientist and not every scientist will be able to inspire young students. Some projects funded by the Pulse initiative were not as successful as anticipated because scientists and artists were not able to develop a fruitful dialogue. As hard as it might be, it is probably as important for these 'failed' encounters to be documented and evaluated as some of the more obviously successful ones. It could be here that the most significant learning will be found.

Creative encounters are necessarily collective rather than individual achievements. The collective also necessarily needs to include different skills and different ways of seeing the world. These might be divided by generation, discipline, cultural background or language. Not only does this contribute to the assessment challenges, but this also means there will inevitably be communication difficulties and misunderstanding. The biggest successes are generally achieved not by a consistent and cosy level of agreement but by accommodations, tolerance, persuasion and occasionally agreeing to disagree. It may not be a process of consensus but one of productive tensions.

Creative encounters will not be easy to measure and will present serious challenges for many forms of evaluation used by policy makers and assessment prevalent in formal education. This is in part due to their tendency for collective, rather than individual, activity, the mixture of subjective and objective approaches and the bringing together of different value systems. This will need to be addressed in a number of ways. It demands innovation on the parts of educators and policy makers to develop means of assessment versatile enough to deal with complex learning outcomes. This in itself might require a high level of interdisciplinary collaboration. It requires sensitivity on the part of artists and scientists to the pressures on educators. Perhaps this also means there should be sensitivity on the parts of educators to the pressures on policy makers – but not too much sensitivity.

In the introduction and in the articles, this book has tried to illustrate some commonalities in which creative encounters can be recognised: where there is both dialogue and productive tensions between collaborators and participants, where there are new, shared and sometimes strange ways of seeing the world prompted possibly by participants responding to limiting definitions, where there is a collective realisation of the need for change.

A creative encounter is thus often about the questioning of authoritative opinion, and the social consequences that flow from such entrenched ways of looking at the world. The transgendered young people in Catherine McNamara and Alison Rooke's article expose the inadequacies of conventional medical definitions of gender and envision means of collective support and self-realisation. In Angela Calabrese Barton and Tara O'Neill's piece, young people in a deprived inner-city neighbourhood disembed science from their school and take it onto the streets. Projects such as these draw attention to the limits of science and science education, and open opportunities for fresh collaborations between scientists and artists to provide a richer and more complete understanding of life-as-lived.

Creative encounters might take place in classrooms, laboratories and theatres. They might just as well take place in former underwater weapons establishments or virtual worlds. Learning spaces will need to change or be reimagined, but as Stephen Heppell points out, there are grounds for optimism and these changes will happen. Schools will continue to be important sites for creative encounters but the boundaries of physical spaces will need to adapt alongside the boundaries of disciplinary spaces. When some young people have, for whatever reason, become disillusioned by traditional learning spaces or contexts, creative encounters in unconventional learning spaces may enable them to reconnect on their own terms. Calabrese Barton and O'Neill's example refers to young people "reauthoring their own place in the world of science". Through their video project the students ended up doing some activities which might be considered to be fairly traditional school science, but the change of context – time and space – was enough to change their relationship to the activity.

Creative encounters happen when scientists, artists, educators and young people permit themselves and each other a sense of wonder. The famed 'wow' factor can still be found in science and art. Moments of revelation seem to be at the heart of Beau Lotto's work on how illusions can help students 'redefine normality' and Joe Winston's discussion of science theatre for children, which aimed not so much to explain but to inspire awe, charm or encourage play. It works both ways. A scientist involved in All Change Arts' *Skin Deep* project brought on board to give some advice on the accuracy of science content ended up contributing his artistic as well as scientific opinion to the project, not to mention more time than he originally planned, and discovered a passion for and wonder at theatre, not just as a means of science communication but for its own sake. He is still involved with the organisation several years and projects later. The denial of this instinctive sense of wonder risks leaving scientists without their passion and students shorn of their curiosity.

Creative encounters may be deeply surreal and involve hybrid dolls, dancing synapses and ghostly pillow-headed figures. However, they also need a root in real human experience, a sense that they have a real or important rationale or an authenticity outside the context of the learning situation. This could be found in the moving personal narrative inspiring the art work, such as the story told by the young man with cystic fibrosis who initiated the *Visiting Time* project at Dorset County Hospital, or the experience of the group of transgendered young people. It could be related to the very excitement of working with a cutting-edge area of science such as epigenetics. Or it could lie in the social space of public performance or exhibition.

Creative encounters may well be a luxury, the icing on the cake of robust disciplinary knowledge. However, the world changes fast and it could also be that challenges such as climate change need our intellectual and human resources to work in new, flexible and ever-shifting configurations. In what Manuel Castells (2000) calls "the network society" where social connections cross geographical and disciplinary borders in all directions, soon (or even now) a writer in Kenya might be collaborating with an epidemiologist in the UK and a social scientist in Brazil to empower communities in all three places to respond to the health consequences of climate change. This collaboration will require on all their parts an ability to make sense of the world in different ways. In an afterword to Castells, echoing the educational theory of Jerome Bruner, Rosalind Williams (2004) makes the point that: "One of the fascinating complexities of the human mind is the persistent coexistence of two very different modes of structuring human experience: through logic and through narrative." Both of these modes are needed interchangeably in facing up to the implications of new problems and new technologies collectively and creatively. Providing opportunities for young people to experience creative encounters today may mean they recognise them when they need them tomorrow.

Bibliography

Castells M. The Rise of the Network Society. Oxford: Blackwell; 2000.

Williams R. Afterword to Castell's The Network Society: A cross-cultural perspective: An historian's view. http://web.mit.edu/~rhwill/www/writing/castells-afterword.html [accessed 29 April 2008].

Biographies

Elio Caccavale, born 1975 in Naples, Italy, studied product design at Glasgow School of Art before going on to the Royal College of Art to complete a Master's in Design Products. His research projects involve collaborations with scientists, social scientists and bioethicists.

Elio is a visiting lecturer on the MA Design Interactions course at the Royal College of Art. He holds visiting research positions in: the Interaction Research Studio (Design Department) at Goldsmiths, University of London; the School of Systems Engineering–Cybernetics at the University of Reading; and the Institute of Biomedical Engineering, Imperial College London.

He has exhibited his work and lectured internationally. Most notably, he has presented his work at the World Forum on Science and Civilization organised by the James Martin Institute (part of the University of Oxford). From February to May 2008, his work was exhibited in the *Design and the Elastic Mind* exhibition at the Museum of Modern Art in New York.

Angela Calabrese Barton is an Associate Professor of Teacher Education at Michigan State University. Before moving to MSU in 2006, Angela was on the faculty at Teachers College for nine years. She has been a chemistry teacher, and has developed and taught in numerous after-school programmes for urban youth located in community centres, shelters and schools. Her research, teaching and service intersect around two main themes: (a) science learning and frameworks for unpacking deep engagement; and (b) teacher learning around the intersections of science teaching and youth lives.

She has received a number of awards during her academic career, including: the 2005 American Education Research Association Division K Award for Exemplary Research; the Early Career Research Award, National Association for Research in Science Teaching, 2000; Kappa Delta Pi Research Award (Teaching and Teacher Education), AERA, Division K, 1999; Early Career Award, National Science Foundation, 1998–2003; National Academy of Education Spencer Fellow, 1996–98. Her work appears in books and journals, including the *Educational Researcher*, the *American Education Research Journal*, the *Journal of Research in Science Teaching*, the *Journal of Teacher Education* and *Science Education*.

Kerry Chappell is part-time Research Fellow for the Dance Partners for Creativity (investigating creativity and partnership with dance artists and secondary school teachers) and Aspire (empowering educational change through student voice and participation) research projects at the School of Education of Lifelong Learning, University of Exeter. Kerry's work in both projects incorporates collaborative research with education/arts professionals.

As an Associate of the Centre for Urban and Community Research at Goldsmiths, University of London, Kerry simultaneously works on the Creative Impact Project. She also works on various freelance projects, and lectures and supervises at the University of Exeter, Laban and The Place. With a background as a freelance dance artist and arts education partnership broker, Kerry still works as a dance artist when the opportunity arises, as well as practising aikido (currently Nidan).

Sara J Downham, before moving to South Devon in 2006, lived and worked as an artist and teacher in a number of places in Britain and overseas. These experiences shaped her as both a person and a working artist. Her paintings have been described as "unusual and vibrant orchestrations of colour and form" aimed to intrigue and feast the eyes.

Sara has exhibited widely in Britain, Europe and the USA. She studied Fine Art in London and Manchester and Art History postgraduate studies at Glasgow University. In the late 1980s she was awarded a postgraduate scholarship to paint in Gdansk in Poland for three years, followed by a few months in Budapest. Her art lecturing has taken her as far afield as Australia, Chile, Estonia, North America and Russia.

Stephen Heppell runs his own policy and learning consultancy, Heppell.net Ltd, which is at the heart of innovative learning policy and practice in a host of countries. As a university professor he retains chairs in New Media and in New Learning Environments, and has a remit for horizon-scanning to guide UK Government policy.

As Chairman of LP+ Stephen is currently developing a Chinese language learning community for 20 million Chinese school students, in partnership with China's Sun New Media corporation.

In the 1980s, Stephen founded Ultralab, which became Europe's leading learning technology research centre with projects that pioneered multimedia CD-ROMs and online communities.

He sits on a number of committees, from the British Academy of Film and Television Arts's Film Committee to his chairmanship of the charity the Inclusion Trust, whose team are engaged in transforming the lives of excluded school students, many on the margins of social inclusion. Stephen regularly appears on TV, radio and in printed media around the world.

Anna Ledgard is a producer, researcher and curriculum and professional development leader with 25 years' experience shaping collaborative participatory arts practice with schools, arts, health and cultural organisations. Her main interest is in the facilitation of arts learning partnerships across disciplines and sectors and the professional development of artists and educationalists. Recent work includes arts and science participatory theatre projects *Visiting Time* (2004) and *Boychild* (2007) with artist Mark Storor and the co-devising of innovative professional development programmes such as TAPP (Teacher Artist Partnership Programme) and Eastfeast in London and the East of England.

Ralph Levinson taught science for 12 years in comprehensive schools and sixth-form centres in London before teaching at the Open University and subsequently the Institute of Education, University of London. He has had a long-standing research interest in interdisciplinary links between science and the arts and the teaching of socioscientific issues, and was co-author of the influential *Valuable Lessons* report. He is also a published short story writer.

Beau Lotto is a neuroscientist at University College London. He has pioneered new ways of comparing, contrasting and uniting arts and science. His work on vision is of a high artistic and scientific quality, but is also accessible for a range of audiences on many different levels. Beau has written and lectured widely on the nature of perception; public works include an outdoor six-metre tower of glass, light and solar panels on one of east London's most prominent streets, installation of light, glass and bees for the Science Gallery's *Lightwave* in Dublin in 2008, 'Why is the Sky Blue' for the Serpentine Gallery, 'White Shadows' for the Hayward Gallery (part of the Dan Flavin retrospective), and an exhibition of visual illusion for the Bristol Science Museum. By bridging the gap between the biological sciences, psychology, architecture and visual art, Beau's work provides a platform for us to discover and question everyday notions of the natural world and our place within it.

Catherine McNamara was Course Leader of the MA Applied Theatre at Central School of Speech and Drama before taking up the post of Deputy Dean of Studies there. She was Project Coordinator for 'Sci:dentity – What's the science of sex and gender?', a 12-month Wellcome Trust-funded project that worked with trans and non-trans young people under 22, exploring gender and sexed identities through creative means. Catherine's work has also included practical research into the benefits of voice workshops for trans men.

Catherine's areas of research include gender and performance, and applied theatre practice. Recent publications include 'Re-inhabiting an uninhabitable body: interventions in voice production with transsexual men' in *Research in Drama Education* (2007) and 'Transmale masculinities in performance: subcultural narratives laid bare' in *Alternatives Within the Mainstream II: British postwar queer theatres* (Cambridge Scholars Press, 2007).

Helen Nicholson is Reader in Drama and Theatre at Royal Holloway, University of London, where she specialises in applied drama and contemporary theatre. She works as a researcher and theatre practitioner in educational and community contexts both locally and internationally. She contributes to partnerships between schools and human rights organisations in the Cape Flat townships in South Africa and in 2008 is directing a children's theatre festival in Miraha, Japan. Most recently, her collaboration with Age Exchange Theatre Trust has taken reminiscence theatre to local care homes for the elderly. Helen is co-editor of the journal *Research in Drama Education*, published by Routledge. Her most recent books include *Applied Drama: The gift of theatre* (Palgrave, 2005) and, with Emma Govan and Katie Normington, *Making a Performance: Devising histories and contemporary practices* (Routledge, 2007). She is currently working on a new book, *Theatre & Education*, to be published in 2009.

Tara O'Neill is the Director of Science and 7th-grade science teacher at Isaac Newton Middle School for Math and Science in New York City, USA. Tara began her career in education as a high-school teacher. She taught 9th-grade physical science, 10th-grade biology and 11th/12th-grade anatomy and physiology in Winthrop, Massachusetts. In September 2001, Tara moved to New York City to pursue her PhD in Science Education at Teachers College, Columbia University. In her current role of Director of Science Tara has been able to capitalise on her experience both as a classroom teacher and as an education researcher. In autumn 2008, Tara is moving to Hawaii to serve as an Assistant Professor of Teacher Education at the University of Hawaii, Manoa. Her research, teaching and service intersect around two main themes: science learning and frameworks for unpacking deep student engagement, specifically, how students can and do develop a sense of ownership in science learning and how this affects their desire to participate in science; and teacher learning and practices that support the development of teacher and student agency.

Simon Parry works at the Wellcome Trust and is currently leading on the development of an international public engagement programme. The new programme focuses on supporting engagement between health researchers and communities in developing countries affected by the research. Simon previously worked within the Trust's young people's education and arts programmes, managing a range of initiatives to promote creative or informal approaches to stimulating discussion about the impact of science on society. He set up and managed the Pulse funding initiative, which funded a series of innovative young people's arts projects inspired by biomedical science. Alongside his work at the Trust, Simon is pursuing his own research into the way drama in community and educational contexts explores notions of citizenship.

Anthony Pinching is Associate Dean for Cornwall and Professor of Clinical Immunology at Peninsula Medical School. He is an active clinician, working mainly with people with CFS/ME, and previously also people with HIV/AIDS. In both arenas he has also been involved in public policy and development of services, as well as advising patient support groups. He has had a substantial research portfolio in both areas and remains an active teacher. Involvement in the medical humanities (music, drama, poetry) – to help students develop their understanding of the art of medicine – has enabled him to explore in a fresh way the wider personal and social impact of disease, making sense of what he has learned from patients.

Michael Reiss is Professor of Science Education at the Institute of Education, University of London, Director of Education at the Royal Society, Chief Executive of Science Learning Centre London, Honorary Visiting Professor at the University of York, Docent at the University of Helsinki, Director of the Salters-Nuffield Advanced Biology Project, a member of the Farm Animal Welfare Council and Editor of the journal *Sex Education*. His research and consultancy interests are in science education, bioethics and sex education. Recent books of his include *Teaching about Scientific Origins: Taking account of creationism* (2007, with L Jones), *Learning Science Outside the Classroom* (2004, with Peter Lang and M Braund), *Key Issues in Bioethics: A guide for teachers* (2003, with Ralph Levinson), *Values in Sex Education: From principles to practice* (2003, with J M Halstead) and *Understanding Science Lessons: Five years of science teaching* (2000). For further information see www.reiss.tc.

Alison Rooke is a lecturer and researcher in the Sociology Department, Goldsmiths, University of London. Her research interests include class, gender and sexualities in urban contexts. She has written on issues relating to cosmopolitanism, visibility, embodiment and belonging in classed and queer cultures. She is particularly interested in gendered and sexual subjectivities, and empirical research that grounds queer theorising in everyday lived complexity.

Alison's PhD research, 'Lesbian landscapes and portraits: the sexual geographies of everyday life', was a visual ethnography exploring the interconnections of spatiality and subjectivity for working-class lesbian and bisexual women.

Alison was responsible for the evaluation of the Sci:dentity project. This built on her interest and track record in participative action research and evaluation in national and European contexts, with a specific focus on developing creative methodologies for demonstrating the social, economic and cultural impact of the arts.

Dave Strudwick qualified as a teacher in 1990, having studied at Rolle College, Devon. He has been a class teacher and a special educational needs coordinator, and ran a group for primary-school-aged children who had been permanently excluded from their previous school. His version of learning is about seeing things differently, whether that is about the Tudors or what makes us each tick.

This led onto him becoming an advisory teacher for behaviour and then into developing 'Healthy Schools' in Devon. During this time he co-authored a book about helping children that challenge us to learn. Dave has since become a headteacher in a small rural primary school in the village of Blackawton, where the emotional health of children and adults has a high priority.

Jeff Teare has over 35 years of major theatre credits to his name, ranging from associate directorships with the Young Vic and the Theatre Royal Stratford East in London through to a wide variety of productions from Penzance to Newcastle. He has been involved with over 150 school science/drama projects and many workshops, readings and professional productions with the specialist consultancy Tinderbox (which he co-founded with Rebecca Gould in 2002) and Theatrescience.

Simon Turley is both a teacher and a prolific writer. His work has been produced by the Theatre Royal Plymouth, Paines Plough, the BBC and the Barbican Theatre, and he scripted Plymouth's *Our Town Story* for the Millennium Dome. Some of his issue-based work has focused on risk and substance abuse, mental health matters and parenting. He has played a key role in the development of Theatrescience through writing, and through designing, trialling and implementing the project's innovative education workshops.

Joe Winston is currently Associate Professor (Reader) in Drama and Theatre Education at the University of Warwick, where he coordinates the MA in Drama and Theatre Education and is Director of Research Degrees. Previously he taught in primary/middle schools and was a head teacher. He has published widely in the field of drama education, where his publications include *Drama, Narrative and Moral Education* (RoutledgeFalmer, 1998) and *Beginning Drama 4–11* (David Fulton Press, co-authored with Miles Tandy), the third edition of which will appear in 2008. He is also co-editor of the international journal *Research in Drama Education*. Recently he has become interested in the idea of beauty and its potential to inform educational discourse. His book *Beauty and Education* will be published by Routledge in 2009.